GET OFF YOUR ARSE & GRAB THAT NEW JOB

STRAIGHT-TALKING ADVICE
ON HOW TO GET THE
PERFECT CAREER

Steve Miller

headline

Copyright © 2009 Steve Miller Training Ltd

The right of Steve Miller to be identified as the Author of
the Work has been asserted by him in accordance with the
Copyright, Designs and Patents Act 1988.

First published in 2009 by
HEADLINE PUBLISHING GROUP

1

Cataloguing in Publication Data is available from the British Library

ISBN 978 07553 1772 1

Typeset in Bell MT by Ben Cracknell Studios

Printed and bound in the UK by CPI Mackays, Chatham ME5 8TD

Headline's policy is to use papers that are natural, renewable and recyclable products
and made from wood grown in sustainable forests. The logging and manufacturing
processes are expected to conform to the environmental regulations of the country of
origin.

HEADLINE PUBLISHING GROUP
An Hachette Livre UK Company
338 Euston Road
London NW1 3BH

www.headline.co.uk
www.hachettelivre.co.uk

This book is dedicated to the memory of my inspiration and special friend June Linda Thompson who sadly passed away in April 2007. There-is not a single day that passes when you are not in my thoughts. Grief fades but the memories don't. Onward and upwards, darling!

CONTENTS

Contents

Acknowledgements

Thanks to the professionals who made it happen:

My lawyer Jason Straford-Lysandrides and the legal team that supports him
The team at Headline, especially my publishers Jo Roberts-Miller and
Wendy McCance and my publicist Emily Furniss
Eddie Bell, an outstanding agent
The PR team at PH Media
Jean Wilde and Matt Rowlands for their creative genius

And, of course, to my personal friends, of whom there are too many to
mention. You know who you are.

But finally to:
Alan Possart for making life perfect
Terry Brookes for being who you are
My fabulous mum and dad, and my niece and nephew, Amy and Ryan

Introduction

Life change is now part and parcel of everyday life in the twenty-first century, which means you really don't know what's around the corner today or tomorrow. So your arse well and truly needs to have smoke coming out of it because you are going to have to move with the fast pace of life. If you just stand still then it's going to be virtually impossible to have the standard of living and the lifestyle you deserve.

This book will give you the kick up the backside you need to grab hold of the career that you feel should be yours, but you've been too scared, lazy or confused to take the first step. It will inspire you to take charge of your future right now, and not leave things up to fate which in my view can be 'fatal'.

I'm going to give you insights, advice and practical tips based on my successful career in human resources, sales and as a straight-talking lifestyle motivator.

I guess I really found that I clicked with people and had a genuine interest in them and their needs when I worked as a holiday camp entertainment rep. Yes, I was a Butlins Redcoat and loved every minute of it. I got close enough to many different people to find out what really makes them tick and what keeps them happy. It stood me in good stead as my career progressed to helping others to develop aspects of their professional and private lives.

Spells in sales and a customer service directorship underlined where my passions really were and led me to develop my career by moving into human resource management.

I fondly remember a project I undertook in my mid-20s for West Midlands Police. This was to be my first taste of recruiting and selecting staff and it was a real eye-opener for me. One of my key projects was to recruit people for a role that many would regard as the lowest of the low – traffic warden. I thought who on earth would want to do a job that brought you into daily conflict with almost everyone, from the most placid pensioner to genuinely bad people? I was amazed at the volume of applicants; there were hundreds of people from all walks of life. Still, to this day, that remains the most popular job I recruited for. Perhaps it was the uniform, or people just like the idea of the power and authority that a traffic warden can have!

I also worked for Grosvenor Casinos for a time, heading up their human resource function for the north of England. The experience it gave me was huge as the people who work in this area of the leisure industry are very colourful. One day would see me dealing with a case of sexual harassment and the next conducting interviews for graduate trainees. The people were wonderful, full of personality, individuality and character.

I then moved on to work for the Trader Media Group and eventually came to lead their training function and the HR team developing professional recruitment practices and employee relations. This included training managers and directors in professional interviewing and assessment skills. It was in this role that I had personal responsibility for recruiting at all levels of the organisation. One day I would be planning an assessment centre for graduates, and the following day would see me recruiting a senior manager and then maybe company accountants. The recruitment aspect of my job was very broad and I loved every minute of it. It was a busy role which I found both stimulating and challenging and it was wonderful leading a team of dedicated HR professionals.

My experience tells me, without doubt, that the quality of job applicants in the UK has deteriorated and much more needs to be done to improve the skills and personal qualities of people in the job market. I believe there is a range of reasons for this. First, there's a lack of commitment to embrace lifelong learning to develop skills and behaviours. The second is the weakness of interpersonal skills and the ability of applicants to sell themselves. I recall interviewing an applicant who on his CV looked the ideal fit for a senior management role. On meeting him not only did this applicant look as if he needed a good wash, but the only thing his communication skills inspired in me was the wish for a good night's sleep. It may be that people are relying on CV templates and then stretching the truth too much on their CV to make themselves shine. I believe employers tend to see through any bullshit straight away and that if you over-egg your CV to look flash and stand out from the crowd then you will get caught out.

The third and perhaps most worrying symptom of the crap quality of job candidates is their general lack of ambition. I know of many employers who are struggling to recruit people who have oomph, career focus and drive.

The good news is that my experience and no-bull style will get you into shape to become a sharp job candidate. This book is full of practical straight-talking advice on how you can get out there, get off your arse and grab the job of your dreams. Whether you are a city worker facing redundancy, a manager looking to move upwards, or a woman looking to return to work after a career break to bring up the kids, this book will give you real inspiration and focus. It will get you to assess your skills, align them to the ideal job and show you how to inspire at interview with outstanding confidence. But remember, the book is only half of it. You also need to get off your arse and go and grab that new job.

If this is the first time you've come across me then be prepared for some frank, honest and fun steps that will take you through the whole process of landing the job you really want. Let's get on with it.

Job for life – forget it!

1

We all know that the days of 'a job for life' are well and truly gone. You and I appreciate that organisations can't and don't work like that any more, so forget the dreams of getting your 'gold watch' from a firm which really values your loyalty and commitment.

The pattern now in the workplace is to have 'serial careers'. For example, graduates can expect to have at least three career changes during their 40-year working life and often it's quite a few more than three. This is a simple statistical fact that doesn't take into account all the variable factors that impact on you and your career, from office politics that force you out to economic uncertainty and company failures. It's a minefield out there.

As well as the constant turmoil of our lives impacted on by our own decisions, and the forces out of our control, there are very significant pressures to be a success at what we do to make a living. Not only are the expectations of our peers high, but those of our children are downright unrealistic. Let's face it, little Peter wants to be the next

Steven Gerrard and little Jane wants to be the next Leona Lewis. Our kids are getting preoccupied with careers that attract fame, money and 'happiness', but in reality they are only ever going to be within the grasp of a talented few. You've also got to ask the question: are these celebrities any more happy than someone working in retail or accounting? Probably not, because, just like you and me, they have to deal with the major ups and downs of life, but with the added pressure of doing it under the media spotlight. The message is simple; think about what you want from your job, keep your expectations real and ignore the 'perfect perceptions' of others.

In contrast to those people whose expectations are simply unrealistic, there are many who will not realise their ambition simply because they are lazy and are not prepared to push themselves. I've personally seen plenty of people who could go on to great things in the commercial world, but just couldn't be arsed to put their hand up and take the initiative. There's such a waste of real talent and prospects; if you think you've got it, then flaunt it.

Living with change

Learning to live with change is difficult for most people, but I want enjoying the challenge of change to be the starting point in you grabbing that new job. It's no good standing still and wrapping yourself in a career just because it feels comfy and safe. That's deathly dull and, to be honest, it's what I expect of a loser – but you're not a loser because you are reading this book.

Change when it comes to your job doesn't necessarily mean ditching your current post and going elsewhere. It could also be about you changing your job's responsibilities, for example by taking on more senior duties. I am aware of hundreds of people who have started on the shop floor and moved on in their careers and reached the board room. Just think about the example of Sir Ken Morrison, who took Morrisons supermarkets from regional mediocrity to become a major player in the UK's multiple retail sector; or across the pond, look at Sam Walton who started as a trainee with J.C. Penney and went on to found the Wal-Mart empire in 1962.

Ask yourself why you want to change your job. Is it to get more back in terms of personal satisfaction, better money, greater respect or a combination of these reasons? Identify in your mind why you want to take this important step to change your life and write down your personal goals and aspirations when it comes to your job. A word of advice: you have to be realistic; if for example your ultimate goal is to earn a lot of money quickly, don't expect to cobble a CV together and get a job as a hedge fund manager. It ain't gonna happen. Match your aspirations with your skills, talent, experience and qualifications.

If you want to be successful, then embrace change and break that natural habit of fearing things that are unknown, unexpected and new.

There are too many excuses for you to pull out for not being able to 'get on' in your current role or to look for new opportunities. There are more and more chances to climb the corporate ladder with larger organisations actively 'talent spotting' to find their next tiers of managers and directors.

I know full well that there are plenty of training opportunities for those who are bothered to get off their arse, and the hype about the restricted access to university courses is complete rubbish; let's face it, university isn't always the answer to building a rewarding career. Yes, the access might be restricted to the top four or five universities, but that's because they want the cream of the crop.

Running scared of change

If you want to grab that new job then embrace change with open arms and forget the natural fear factor. It's my firm belief that fear simply means **F**alse **E**xpectation **A**ppearing **R**eal. You think you can't land a new job because you're too old, too young, under-qualified, over-qualified, whatever, you are putting false expectations about that new role into your head without giving things a chance to happen.

The typical fears that act as barriers to change can include: not having the right skill set, changing your work environment/location, being scared of a new boss and, of course, the fear of actually not being any good at the interview.

I have good news for you. I am going to explain to you the three fear breakers. These fear breakers will be applied throughout the book, so that you will always be in a strong position to grab that job when opportunities arise.

F**k the fear

1. Boost belief in your brilliance – by learning to take control of your thoughts and, what's more, developing your store of positive beliefs that you are going to be able to work fucking miracles. Consider that your mind is split into two distinct areas – your conscious mind and your unconscious mind. You need to develop a bank of really positive words, pictures and feelings in your unconscious mind as these will determine how you not only perceive change but how you deal with it.

In Chapter 6 you will be given a number of mind workouts to strengthen your self-belief, so that you are able to perform with excellence at the interview and move into your next job role with absolute confidence.

2. *Quit moaning* – I bet a lot of your time is spent sitting with colleagues and moaning about your current job – your boss, the crap money, poor prospects, other colleagues, the journey to work and so on – but you are too scared to move on. From this moment forward just shut your trap and quit moaning, because you are not only boring yourself and compounding your own inaction, but you are probably boring other people as well. Constantly moaning drains you mentally and physically, and the people around you. You'll also begin to be viewed as the whinger who frustrates the pants off everyone around you. So each time you notice you are about to moan, imagine a big muzzle being placed on your gob. You'll be doing yourself and all those around you a real favour.

3. *Act* – You are going to feel so much better if you simply act now. I want you to apply the JFDI principle – Just Fucking Do It. Once you get the ball rolling and you see, feel and hear yourself moving forward, it all starts to get easier. This may be taking initial steps like registering with an employment agency, developing a new CV, or making a phone call to a contact who can advise you on your next job move.

Remember procrastinators are doomed. These are the lazy little shits who usually do nothing, but make sure that they pull down everyone else who is trying to make something of their life by getting off their arse and going for it.

Real life

Richard

Richard was a 26 year old working as an electrician, but after several years he decided he wanted a complete change from this career.

His dream was to put something back into the community where he lives and works on a daily basis. However, he was frustrated by the lack of opportunity to play a caring role in the community and had a passion for helping people with his excellent communication skills. He was looking for something that would feed his need to work with people in his community and also call on his ability to apply practical knowledge and skills.

After some soul searching, research and planning he decided that his life passion had been staring him in the face for some time. That passion was to become a paramedic. Richard had a friend who'd been in a serious road accident and whose life had been saved by a passing paramedic. This had stayed with him for many years. It became the impetus for his determination to become one himself. You may have some moment in your life that changes your perspective on what's important and on what you should be doing as a career. There's no real way of telling you when this is or what it might be, but you will know it if and when it happens.

The first step he took was to get off his arse and find out what training was needed to become a fully qualified paramedic. As a mature student he went to university to do a degree incorporating paramedic science and now at the age of 33, he is a successful paramedic who tells me he is completely satisfied by his job.

Gillian

Gillian was 43 and had three children who were now grown up.

Keeping the house, home and family together had kept Gillian out of the job market for over 20 years and, quite naturally, she had concerns and fears about returning to work.

She came to me to help her deal with the anxieties that were stopping her getting back into the workplace. Our time together was focused on techniques to help boost her self-belief (some simple self-hypnosis which is set out in Chapter 6) and on identifying a set of qualities that we could enhance together to appeal to employers. The qualities we identified were: she's great at negotiating with others, likes to meet people, and has a really good knowledge of food and cookery.

She quickly got her first break and returned to work becoming a part-time waitress, but I knew Gillian quite literally had bigger fish to fry. She had a lot more to offer, so she enrolled in a full-time food and business course at the College of Food in Birmingham. Six years later, she now owns and manages her own successful restaurant.

Janet

After a career as airline cabin crew, Janet decided at the age of 39 to leave the 'friendly skies' behind and try something completely different.

Her experience in customer relations with the airline had developed her talent to influence people, especially in some of the tricky situations that we know can develop on aeroplanes. Janet's problem was that she needed to up her salary quickly because her personal circumstances had changed overnight.

She identified that a career in sales could offer her a good salary base and also the uncapped potential to generate the extra income that she needed.

She performed brilliantly at interview and landed a job as a sales executive with a major publishing group. The organisation suited Janet's ambition and abilities, she performed outstandingly well, and was quickly promoted to become a sales manager.

She helped to plan and set up national publications for her company, and to establish a new and profitable arm for the business. Janet now holds a senior director level position in this leading media and publishing company.

I hope you can see that when it comes to your job and your career ambitions that a change is as good as a rest. Employers now expect that people will have a range of varied backgrounds, some will be academically based, some will have worked their way up and some will have a mix of paper qualifications and on-the-job experience. They will also be happy to see, within reason, that you may have tried one or two career paths and held a few different jobs in the past, but not dozens.

There's everything to gain by embracing change when it comes to your job prospects and career aspirations. I will help you take hold of opportunity and shape you into a product that will wow employers.

At the end of each chapter I want to recap on the major points and recommendations that I have made. Here's your first Job Grabber check list:

Job Grabber *check list*

- Be prepared for change, and to change your job
- Accept change in your career as an opportunity
- Remember successful people have a vision and embrace change
- F**k the fear and grab the opportunities
- Believe in yourself, quit moaning and just do it – grab that new job

The great escape

2

Taking the decision to leave an employer can be really tough, but, on the other hand, for some people it's what they have to do to keep sane, get more money or whatever.

Fear not, because in this chapter I will help you make that decision in a careful and considered way by getting you to read and digest the six 'great escape' job assessment guides. The guides are here to support you in taking stock of what your current role gives you and what may be achieved by moving on. Look at each question carefully before you give your score.

As you work through each assessment you will answer questions based on how much you agree or disagree. Make sure you are as honest with yourself as possible, as this will enable you to base your decision on true feelings and facts. You are required to score each assessment statement from 0 to 5. The lower you score, the less you agree with the statement that's being made. Then add up your five scores for each section and divide by five to give you an average for each assessment. Spend some time doing this, as there is no right or wrong answer; it's about you being true to yourself.

The great escape job assessment tool will help you make that final decision: whether to wave goodbye or sit tight. It's vital that you stay with your job, or decide to ditch it, for the right reasons and motivations, as the decision may have life-changing consequences. For example, if you are unhappy in your role because you have a senior manager who you feel bullies you, then it may be the wrong thing to be forced out by them. If you stick with it, the boss may get fired or transferred, or you might get promoted above them. What I'm saying is that the decision to stay or go should be carefully weighed up and thought through. The great escape tool is a brilliant way to get you thinking straight and it will support you in making a fully informed choice.

Assessment 1: The Security Blanket

- I currently enjoy the feeling of job security
- I have sound relationships with those who determine my future job security
- My face fits and I am confident that I am an asset to my employer
- I am pretty certain that my employer would try and keep me if the threat of redundancies hung over the business
- The organisation is currently in good financial shape

Your Score: ___ /5

Assessment 2: Value Alignment

- My values fit the organisation's ethos closely
- I come to work knowing what my organisation stands for, what it aligns itself to and what I believe and expect in life
- I feel very comfortable because the culture of my employer is just what I expect
- I am proud to be working for my organisation
- My boss has very similar values to myself and this reinforces the close relationship I have with my employer

Your Score: ___ /5

Assessment 3: Mental Stretch and Personal Development

- I find my work stimulating and it is rare that I get bored
- I am coached and developed to learn new skills
- My employer has a positive attitude towards training and development
- I am afforded the opportunity to attend training courses to develop and expand my skill base
- The people around me at work stimulate my mind and I learn from them

Your Score: ___ /5

Assessment 4: Remuneration

- The salary I receive is fair and I am satisfied with the benefits package. (If you're not sure if what you are getting as a package is what the market is paying, then do some research on the internet and look at similar jobs and grades to yours. Consider if you match up, are better off or worse off.)

- The employer rewards effort and would offer an increment to my salary if I exceeded my objectives
- The pension plan offered by the organisation is sound
- When I compare my current salary to similar roles in other organisations there is no doubt that mine is very competitive
- Earning a good salary is important to me and it is highly unlikely I would ever be willing to take a pay cut if I decided to move on

Your Score: ___ /5

Assessment 5: Work/Life Balance

- I enjoy my time with family and friends as well as time at work
- My employer has a good attitude towards flexible working
- My employer would take the request for greater flexibility seriously and do what they could to accommodate my needs
- I would describe my employer as family friendly
- My boss takes an interest in my home life and will assist in supporting me at times of need

Your Score: ___ /5

Assessment 6: My Future Is Bright

- I am reasonably ambitious and it is important to me that my employer helps to meet my ambitions
- I can see a range career progression opportunities with my current employer
- At my annual appraisal my line manager takes time to explore my future prospects

- I really do believe my employer is supporting my personal and professional growth
- I have no doubt in the short to medium term I will be promoted and in the long term my ambitions will be met

Your Score: ___ /5

Grand Total: ___

Your results

0-5: Get out and get a new job immediately. It's fucking serious so before you have a breakdown take my advice and get off your arse and grab that new job right now. Consider resigning today as it's obviously hell for you.

6-10: You must seriously think about changing your job as soon as possible. You are obviously not happy and your needs are not being satisfied. It is highly unlikely that your own requirements will be met for some time so get off your arse this week, get your CV polished, and contact some good employment agencies. Call all your contacts and start networking because it is time to make a move as soon as possible.

11-15: There are real concerns for you at the moment so it is time to look around and market yourself. Assess your skills and make some enquiries to seek out opportunities elsewhere. Sign up with recruitment agencies over the next month and consider all your options. Take your time because whilst it is time to get a new job it's not the red alert situation being faced by our friends above. This is good in a way because it means you can make sure you are well prepared to move on.

16-20: You obviously have some frustrations at the moment and it is worth considering your options. However, consider talking to your line manager about your concerns before you act in haste. As you talk to him or her make sure you stay positive, telling them you want to stay with your current employer and where you see yourself fitting in. Don't start walking around muttering under your breath with a face like a smacked arse as they may think you are becoming a whinge bag. If you talk to your boss/es they may well be able to help so avoid jumping ship because the one you are on may sail to job paradise. If you really feel that things are not going to work out for you where you are then start to meticulously plan your exit strategy.

Over 20: Stop right there Mr/Mrs! Stay where you are! It's not that bad so start to think yourself lucky. Promote your career dreams and ambitions through your current employer and maintain a positive attitude. You might find that promotion comes sooner than you think.

If you have scored yourself in this group I want you to really think hard about how you move forward because there may be things about yourself that you don't know and plans that your employer has that will make you even more willing to stick where you are.

Leaving your job with dignity

Don't be a serial job hopper

The last thing you want on your CV is a list of jobs that you have been unable to hold down. Yes, job hopping is frowned upon by most employers, so be careful. You'll need to explain clearly to any potential new employer why you haven't managed to hold down a job for a decent length of time. Make sure you have good reasons to explain your pogo stick career history. An employer will look at the amount of time you have spent in a job and in my opinion you need to have done a couple of years so that it doesn't look as if you quickly get bored. In ten years you don't want to have had more than three or four jobs, unless it's accepted in the sector or profession you are in.

Sure you will be fine if it was a one off, but if there is a list of unexplained escapes it will make you look dodgy. There are people out there, and some will be reading this book, who can't stick at a job role. If you are one of them then this chapter is so important for you because it will help you to realise that getting the role you really want takes careful planning and consideration.

Leaving a company in less than two years is going to be explored by the interviewer, so make sure you have solid reasons for the rapid exit.

If you are offered a new opportunity internally, then that's something to consider carefully. It needs to be a progression that will add something to the skills and prospects you have. If you are staying where you are in the medium to long term, then seizing promotion opportunities is probably a good thing to do. But be careful that you are committed to the company because if you want to leave then you must do it on good terms. This is all about weighing up where you see yourself in the future and making the right choice to get you where you need to be.

Realistically then, accepting your next job will mean being certain you can commit at least two or three years. If you have been a serial job hopper you are well advised to take some quality time rather than take a job you're not certain is right. Listen to your gut and if you have concerns don't accept the first offer. If you leave too soon, expect hard feelings and no future references.

Talk it over before you exit

Rather than being one of those employees who hides their frustration and becomes bitter and twisted, share your issues and concerns with your line manager. If you really feel as if your job is in a dead end, or you are not receiving the increased responsibility you crave, then be sure to discuss it with your manager. You won't be sacked for highlighting that you want to grow, take on more responsibility and have more opportunity. If you truly feel your position is stagnant or boring and it's not your fault, then for goodness' sake talk about it and give your boss a chance to help put it right.

As you meet with the boss be calm and make sure you provide concrete examples of the problems you face and what the possible solutions are. It's no good throwing loads of problems at them without offering some practical solutions.

If this is done professionally, you may be pleasantly surprised at how helpful and accommodating your boss will be. At the end of the day at least things will be out in the open and you know you have done your best to improve things. If you have a proven positive track record and a good attitude, your position is obviously strengthened. If you want improvement or a promotion simply because you feel entitled to it, without practical examples of achievement, then get real because you probably don't deserve it.

Hunting for a new job at work? Never!

OK, so you have email and internet access at work, but remember this is the property of your employer, and if they have an IT policy it is likely they can access it at any time. So never think that your work email is private. Bearing that in mind, don't be a fool and send off your CV from your work email address and certainly don't be a complete loony and hold telephone interviews on the company phone as logs are often checked.

So, you are not at all as safe as you might think when it comes to you searching for a new job on your current employer's time. Also, remember colleagues love to gossip. If you haven't been open about moving on with your boss, then your remaining days will in all likelihood be very awkward. This is even worse if you get caught out trying to find a new job and they don't know about it. In other words you are probably fucked and any pay increases, bonuses or training programmes that were coming your way will be lost.

Never leave unfinished business

I remember an acquaintance of mine who managed a busy recruitment department for a public sector organisation. The department was responsible for processing all applications, organising interviews, assessment processes and completing administration for issuing new contracts. My colleague was very angry when he was told he was going to be made redundant. He felt used and abused, so decided to put every new offer of employment letter that should have been sent out in a secret file hidden in a cabinet during the final two weeks of his notice period before starting a new job.

As you can imagine, many successful candidates were very concerned that the contracts of employment that had been promised didn't show up. My acquaintance must have thought the revenge at the time was satisfying, but this idiot didn't realise the long-term consequences. Deliberately leaving unfinished business would harm the new recruits for the organisation as well as the departments which were desperate to get off to a good start with their new employees. My acquaintance was found out and became the villain of the department. His reputation was now worse than it ever was and the Director of Human Resources had to reconsider his reference.

The real point here is that you never play silly little games to get one back on an employer who you feel has hurt you. Forget leaving heaps of unfinished business, otherwise you will well and truly end up shit creek without a paddle.

A fair notice period

Unless your working life is so shit that you are nearing breaking point, you should never walk out without notice. Your employer needs to find a decent replacement who has the capabilities to perform the role competently, so be reasonable. You should do your best to work your contractual notice but, if you consider this unreasonable, then sit down and negotiate. Also consider that if you have a new job working for a competitor, it is likely you will be put on gardening leave.

Avoid the child-like approach of throwing your weight around, being cock sure, just because you are leaving. Instead, be the better person and co-operate with your boss. By doing this you will be showing them they are losing a great asset, and you will keep that bridge intact for a possible come back if you wish it. Acting like a dick is no good for your personal and professional credibility, so being reasonable and professional at all times is a must. Your new employer will understand that you can't literally start tomorrow, so be patient and work your notice period.

Now that we have been through the programme of how to execute 'the great escape', or not, depending on your job motivations and current workplace, you are in a position to take the right decision. It will give you a massive rush if you acknowledge it's time to go and you take control of your future. On the other side of the coin, if you step back and take a look at your current employment situation you may feel that the grass is greenest where you are right now. Remember 'fools rush in . . .'

Job Grabber *check list*

- Assess your situation; use the job assessment guide
- Talk things through with your employer if you are considering leaving
- Be reasonable when hunting for a new job and do it on your own time
- Give a fair notice period
- The decision to leave has been carefully considered – is it a green light for the great escape?

Redundancy – opportunity knocks?

3

Shirley Bassey might warble delightfully that diamonds are forever, but you can bet your last penny that a job isn't. Our culture and economy continue to change radically, so no job is for life and redundancy is something that many thousands of employees have to face each year. It could be you next.

I don't want to paint a picture of doom and gloom, but as I write this book I read in the press that 20,000 city workers are facing the axe at a time of economic uncertainty and downsizing. The prospect of serious job losses in a number of developed economies is on the horizon, so don't ignore this prospect or you may get an unpleasant surprise. I want you to be prepared to deal with the situation of facing redundancy and to come out of it with a smile on your face knowing that your future is brighter than orange.

In the workplace, redundancy is a definite risk of the job. Often, as a result of deteriorating market conditions, an assessment of human resource requirements is made and groups of employees find themselves surplus to requirements. Redundancy can come around for many reasons, from the simple to the complex. I worked with a large business that had grown rapidly, probably too quickly, and before long the company was having to move to much larger premises fifty miles away. This resulted in large-scale redundancies because the majority of employees did not want to transfer to the new site. I've also known plenty of people who have faced redundancy because their department was moved overseas and they weren't needed any more. At the other end of the scale, redundancy can come from the complex strategies of global organisations that are trying to gain an edge in a particular market or country. Never be fooled into thinking that the 'R' word won't come knocking on your door.

Being made redundant can be either a truly awful or a truly liberating experience. You may believe it is horrible that there is going to be a downsizing exercise and your name is on the list. It's quite possible that you feel your world is falling apart. That's because you don't have control over what is happening to you. This is a natural reaction for many, but my own view is that you need to pick yourself up quickly and see the 'opportunity knocking'.

The other way of looking at redundancy is to say 'Fuck it, this is happening and it's out of my hands.' Look at it as an opportunity to move a step up with another organisation in your field, or even to completely change your direction. There may be a host of other possibilities that come knocking; if you get redundancy money you can now go travelling, maybe go under the knife and get that tuck and lift you've been desperate for, drive around flirting outrageously in your new sports car, or start your own business. Suddenly, losing your job may not seem such a terrible prospect after all. You can turn it into a very positive experience.

It might be the case that you are currently facing redundancy and have recently found yourself attending consultation meetings to discuss your options as the time arrives for you to leave your current employer. No doubt you will have covered a range of possibilities from retraining or going to university to going it alone as your own boss. Remember, you need to keep your options open and your chin up.

I believe it's really important that you remember that it is your *role* being made redundant and not you. Don't fall into the trap of starting to think that you were not good enough, or you were a poor performer in your job. The redundancy process is normally being driven by the 'number crunchers' and shareholder interests and you are a cost saving. You must not take it personally. If you do feel you have been treated unfairly, then you are entitled to appeal against your selection for redundancy. It could be that you have been chosen as the candidate for redundancy and a colleague has been kept on. If you think this decision was unfair and made on the grounds of your age, sex or race, then you need to follow formal procedure to register your concerns. Write a formal letter of appeal detailing why you believe this to be the case. If you don't get the right answers, then seek legal advice from an employment law specialist, as you may have good grounds for taking your employer to a tribunal or getting extra compensation for being forced out.

Bear this in mind as you manage the emotions being faced with a life change that is likely to have come as a shock.

Manage the announcement

Once the announcement is made, it is essential that you do not react inappropriately. Yelling and shouting at the boss and slandering the organisation are never going to help your cause. If your emotions are tangled, ask politely if you can take some time out to get your head around it. Save your screams and tears until you get home and then let it all out. If you want to shout, then do so in the confines of your own home. If you want to cry, then have a good one. Now is the time to let out all the crap you can, because you are then going to have to get your life back in order. It's simply no good taking a journey into self-pity, because that's not going to help you. I want you to come out of this keeping your integrity and dignity intact, and your resolve to move onwards and upwards at the top of your agenda.

Think through your actions and forget forms of retaliation, as this is never going to help you influence your organisation to offer you a decent severance package or take you back on in the future. Do remember that circumstances change and that they may well need your talents again, so don't burn those bridges by trying to take 'revenge'.

I want you to act professionally and take this as one of life's knocks that you can move on from quickly. We don't do silly little dramas that can only hurt ourselves and others.

Manage the emotions

Dealing with redundancy can be a real trauma, but it is important to manage your emotions, keep them together, and keep them working positively for you, rather than dragging you down. You want your emotions to take you in the right direction, and you definitely want to avoid the self-destruct button. You certainly need to leave your employer on good terms because you want to keep that particular door open.

I don't usually go in for high brow theories and practices, but when it comes to dealing with redundancy I normally apply the

Steve Miller

Kübler-Ross grief cycle. This is an approach to handling grief and trauma developed by Dr Elizabeth Kübler-Ross who wanted to help people come through events like dealing with the death of a loved one. You might think this is using a hammer to crack a walnut, but the reaction to redundancy can be similar to much more traumatic events. The 'grief model' that she developed actually works as a 'change model' that helps people to understand and deal with how they react to a traumatic event.

You need to both understand and act on it, so that you don't do yourself any harm, or harm others come to that! Take note of the proactive approach and, as redundancy is announced, use this approach to deal with it.

The five key stages include:

1 Denial – thinking it won't ever happen to you and suppressing your feelings about unpleasant change by not acknowledging it's going on

2 Anger – the rage that follows when reality finally kicks in and your employer is talking to you about making you redundant

3 Bargaining – the stage where you bargain with your employer in terms of the redundancy and what will happen to you

4 Depression – dealing with the feelings of loss, or not as the case may be

5 Acceptance – realisation kicks in and it is for real and you take onboard the reality of redundancy.

Emotional response to redundancy	Inappropriate reaction	Proactive approach
Denial	• Ignoring that it will really happen to you • Believing it is weeks if not months away and a lot can happen between now and then • Not discussing the redundancy scenario	• Understanding that change does happen • Allowing time for the redundancy situation to sink in
Anger	• Occasional outbursts of anger about the organisation and individuals within it • An attempt to sabotage the redundancy process • 'Shoot the messenger' (normally the line manager)	• Acknowledge it is natural to be angry • Accept the anger and channel it in a healthy way • Recognising that 'blame will leave you lame', so shooting the messenger is unfair and a wasted emotion and might harm you in the long run
Bargaining	• Look in vain for a way out – often too quickly • Failing to listen to what the organisation will offer as alternatives to redundancy and/ or the redundancy package • Resorting to aggressive bargaining techniques such as threats	• Focus on how you can walk away with a win-win solution for you and the organisation • Respecting the redundancy scenario but assertively requesting reasonable severance terms • Understand that there is room for manoeuvre

Emotional response to redundancy	Inappropriate reaction	Proactive approach
Depression	• Final realisation of the inevitable which leads to self-sabotage • Wanting to escape from the world such as by staying in bed, and a withdrawal from friends, family and society	• A realisation the inevitable has occurred and creating a clear goal • Talking through the loss of job, work colleagues and other variables that add to the grief
Acceptance	• Acceptance that it happened and it will never happen again	• A full exploration of new opportunities • Development of actions to move forward • Once actions are identified, immediate steps are taken

Manage your time well

Between the redundancy announcement and the actual day of 'goodbyes', you should be co-operative. This could mean handing over your responsibilities to someone else and showing them the ropes. Don't be a daft shit and try to sabotage the company by doing things like losing data or giving misinformation to whoever is taking over from you.

Make sure you leave notes to help whoever is going to pick up your work, or sit down and brief them fully. Yes, I know it sounds difficult, but you have to act professionally. Again remember you may want to return one day and let's face it you are definitely going to need a good reference.

Get your CV up to date and make it shine by using the guidance and advice set out in Chapter 15. Your employer will fully understand, and should support you with your mission to look for another job. The law requires them to offer you reasonable time off to do so. But don't take the piss. Taking reasonable time off will mean you take a few days a month rather than weeks. At the same time surf the net and search for employment agencies and head hunters. Also, call friends and other people on your network list as they may well be able to recommend you to one of their contacts. It is also worth surfing internet networks such as Linkedin, as you can come across some great opportunities and advice.

If you find yourself sitting with people who have a lot of silly squabbles about their redundancy, walk away. You can do without these drains. If they want to spend valuable time in victim mode, then let them. Keep away. You can do without their unhealthy energy around you. Losers!

Manage your package

Guys, I'm not talking about what you've got downstairs. This is all about using your loaf and what you have upstairs. Before you rush out and spend any redundancy package be aware that it may have to stretch far. I know I talked about splashing out on a sports car earlier, but that's for those of you who already have money tucked away that will carry you through to your next job. Be sensible.

Sure, there is nothing wrong with spending a little on a treat to cheer yourself up, but only a fool would rush out and splurge all the redundancy away. Of course, if you are going to set up your own business, then spend the money on fixed assets such as a computer or a car. But again, before you run off and do so, talk to your business bank manager.

If, on the other hand, you are job hunting, spend some of the dough on good-quality interview suits, accessories, shoes and a decent fragrance. Yes, it is absolutely OK to make yourself gorgeous. It is also worth using some of your redundancy money to pay for some job-related training. If you have an idea of what you want to do next, then my advice is to invest some of the money into worthwhile personal and professional development training to equip you with the skills that employers will bite off your hand for. As for the rest, pop it into the bank account for those rainy days.

As soon as you receive the redundancy cheque, make a list of all the 'must dos' and assign a cost to them. Be sure to budget very carefully. You may receive a fat cheque, but believe me it will soon become thin, so put it to good use. This will help you to plan financially how long you can be out of work for.

To top up your income, consider offering your services on a freelance basis to your old employer, or perhaps take up a part-time job to keep your head well above water.

Explaining redundancy away

Many, many people at all levels are made redundant each year. Fear not, there is no stigma to redundancy, especially if the organisation has relocated, reorganised or gone out of business completely. If quizzed in interview about why you left the last job, sit in a comfortable upright posture and explain that following a downsizing of the organisation your role was one of those chosen to be made redundant.

It is always useful to explain what your previous employer offered you in terms of learning and development, and that you enjoyed your time with the organisation. Never slag off the company. Be professional and positive about your experience, otherwise the interviewer will feel you are a pain in the arse and a moaning victim. Always be honest about the redundancy. Genuine honesty will show the interviewer that you weren't sacked for being pissed on duty or shagging the boss's wife in the back of your car or, more to the point, in his marital bed.

Restoring your lost confidence

The one big thing I will continually remind you of, when it comes to redundancy, is that it is the *job* that is redundant and *not you*. It is so important that you understand and believe this, otherwise you are going to sink faster than the *Titanic* and no one will be able to rescue you.

You have got to believe me when I say that there is an employer out there desperate for your skill set and your specialist experience. With some planning and effort you will find each other. The real point here is to let go of any self-sabotage. That's right, let it go, because it's the *job* and *not you*.

When you have been made redundant it is so important to keep yourself busy. Avoid staying in bed, day-dreaming, snoring and farting, as this is not going to get you anywhere. You have to get up, get out and do it! Hunt the jobs, speak to the recruitment consultants and turn yourself into a valuable commodity. In between hunting the job opportunities, keep yourself occupied. Perhaps finish off some jobs in the house, get fit, and most of all learn something new. If opportunities haven't come up straight away, then you could consider doing some voluntary work. This will give you something that can keep you sharp and active, and also provide something to talk about at the next interview. It will show a prospective new employer that you get off your arse and use your initiative. This is about making yourself positive and interesting.

Maintain that positive attitude about yourself, but if it isn't very positive at the moment shut up and work again from the start of the book to find the self-belief and determination you are lacking. In other words make yourself positive. Look to the future with a plus sign on your forehead rather than a minus.

Real life

Angela

Angela was a 33-year-old financial analyst working in the City of London. She was highly qualified with six years' service under her belt and earning very good money.

The downturn in the economy led to a downsizing of the business where she was working and Angela was unfortunately made redundant. The silver lining was that Angela's employer offered her the opportunity to have my support to get her into shape to get through the redundancy and move onwards positively.

In our first session, Angela let out her anger: she shouted and cried a little, but acted like an adult and held herself together. She understood that she had to maintain a professional attitude and was determined to leave on good terms with her reputation intact.

In addition, Angela and I planned how she would manage her time up to and after the redundancy. This included identifying and setting her the goal of relocating to the Midlands, prioritising the actions to meet that goal and carrying out the immediate tasks.

Angela was a shining example of how to manage the emotions of redundancy, set a vision and achieve a life-changing goal. She now lives near Warwick and has set up her own business consultancy.

Martin

A 29-year-old sales manager, Martin was given a redundancy notice after three years with the same telecommunications company. The reason for the redundancy, his letter explained, was relocation of the operation to Asia.

For Martin this was a bolt from the blue and really knocked his confidence hard. One of his friends recommended that he contact me for some motivation sessions.

When I met him, I knew straightaway that his major problem was that he was being consumed by his own self-pity. He'd say things like, 'How the hell am I going to survive this? They don't care about anything except protecting the bottom line.' He talked like a victim and felt the world owed him something, but, my dears, we all know that business is business and the needs of individuals rarely count.

He needed my no-nonsense approach and he got a verbal slapping to get him to come to his senses. I gave Martin a kick up the arse and in no uncertain terms I told him to quit being a victim and get with the programme. Initially Martin was defensive, but he soon realised it was time to let go of self-pity and grow up to be a Get Off Your Arse role model.

He made himself busy with new interests — for example he'd always dreamed of being a fossil hunter, so he joined a local amateur archaeology group, sought new employment opportunities, and explained away his redundancy with confidence at interviews.

His confidence soared quickly and within six weeks of being made redundant he was appointed as a senior sales manager with a leading IT software business. He had increased his salary and got the opportunity to travel all over the world, enjoying his work and boosting his fossil collection.

It was a great day for both of us when he called me, thanking me for kicking his arse so hard that he found it difficult to sit down at all now because he was so much more action driven and positive.

Job Grabber *check list*

- Deal with the redundancy notice
- Get your emotional balance sorted
- Use your time to turn it into a positive outcome
- Negotiate your redundancy package and look after it
- Give a fair notice period
- Move on confidently – grab the opportunity

Is it the job you really, really want?

I bet this is a million-dollar question for many of you. 'What do I really want to do next?' you ask yourself. To which you answer, 'I haven't got a bloody clue.'

It's a frustration of many, so be assured you are not alone. However, you have to get your mind into gear and identify what it is you really want at some point, so cut out any unnecessary moaning.

There are practical considerations to be made which we will run through in this chapter, and also there is intuitive information you can retrieve from your most important muscle, your brain. More than you realise, your mind can definitely guide you to find out what it is you really want to do. If you think this is bollocks, then relieve your ignorance and read what I have to say because you will be surprised.

Your intuition is your ally if you allow it to be, and if you let it guide you to the right job, then perhaps you won't fuck up again by making a mistake. It can also take you to the right job if you are returning to the labour market after a break or are a graduate getting your first job.

Consider and complete the following questions to help you identify the career/job move that will set your world on fire, make you leap out of bed each morning and put a big smile on your face.

Make notes after each question to help determine the direction you need to go in. Making the notes is important, as you will need to map out where you will be going and I don't want you to forget or ignore any of my messages.

Six questions to help you decide

Question 1: What are my values?

Start with your values: the things that make you feel happy, content and at your best. Are your values to do with earning lots of money, material assets and status? Or maybe your values are security, good health, and solid relationships? One value is not better than another. It is your choice. Understanding what you value most is the key step to ascertaining what career or job move to make.

Your values need to be aligned to your choice of job role and the culture within which you will work. For example, if you value ambition, money, creativity and attaining results, then typical job roles suited to you may be working in a sales and marketing environment, giving a career that will offer you an obvious ladder to reach the top.

Or take a close friend of mine, Brendan, who valued integrity, the environment and family. He decided to take a role as a tree surgeon. This role met his passion for the environment, and the organisation he worked for was located close to home so he could have regular contact with his family.

Write down here your top three values for life/work. Think through job roles and business cultures that will align themselves to your values.

1 _____

2 _____

3 _____

Question 2: What job fits my personality?

As with your values, your personality style should lend itself to your selected career. I prefer to look at personality in four distinct colours, those being red, green, yellow and blue. This is based on the work of Carl Gustav Jung who was one of the pioneers of modern psychology in the twentieth century. He categorised people's personality type according to simple criteria, and to do this he saw four main archetypes, explained in the figure below. Plot yourself where you see yourself fitting and then read the personality descriptions. When selecting a new job be sure it fits your personality type. Please never try to be something you are not. Be true to yourself. Faking your true personality is exhausting and you may well end up falling flat on your face – so be you!

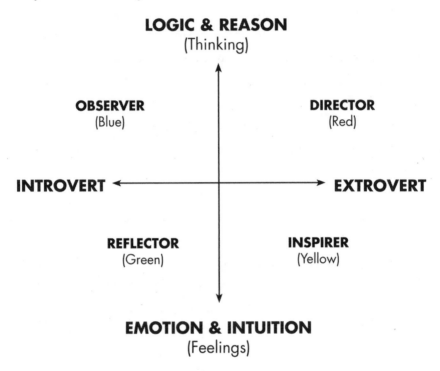

The figure above indicates the two main factors:

i. How people tend to make decisions (represented by the vertical axis)

ii. How people relate to others (represented by the horizontal axis)

From the figure you can see that people will range from those who base decisions on pure logic and reason to those who predominantly take action based on their feelings or 'gut' instinct. It also shows that people will range from those who are outgoing and extrovert, to those who prefer introspection and who are introverts.

Think where you fit best, then consider your personality type as detailed below:

Type 1 – The Director (Red)

A red personality is one that is pretty direct and occasionally somewhat forceful. Reds know what they want and they go all out to get it. In all likelihood they like a professional working environment and don't suffer fools gladly. Achievement is really important to reds, they have no time for waffle and usually enjoy a target-driven culture.

Obvious job roles: sales, business development, account management, entrepreneur, business manager, board director

Type 2 – The Observer (Blue)

Blues enjoy detail and are like pigs in shit if the job involves facts and figures. Blues are often the quieter, thoughtful type, who is less likely to act with the same self-assurance or self-confidence as a red. They will prefer to advise and consult. They don't welcome too much risk or challenge.

Obvious job roles: research, accountancy, proof reader, data analyst

Type 3 – The Inspirer (Yellow)

Yellows are emotional people who will often act on a strong idea or inspiration, energised by the belief that it feels right. Yes, they can be impulsive and unpredictable, as well as creative and highly inspirational. They are people-orientated and enjoy being the centre of attention, the one in the 'limelight'.

Obvious job roles: presenter, teacher, trainer, entertainer

Type 4 – The Reflector (Green)

The greens are also emotional individuals, driven massively by what they feel. Greens are sensitive to others, and always interested in others. They value relationships highly. Being accepted is important to them. They may not be overly insecure, but nevertheless enjoy comfort and safety and dislike too much pressure. Greens tend not to be motivated by the desire to lead. They are also great listeners, and may sometimes show submissive tendencies.

Obvious job roles: nurse, counsellor, customer service executive, facilitator

Clearly we don't all fit into just one of the categories that Jung identified, but we will have strong elements of one that will outweigh others, and this will be the character trait that drives a lot of the decisions you make and how you come across to other people. Once you have plotted where you are, you will have a better understanding of the type of career or job that really should float your boat. So sail away!

Question 3: Do I want to lead or follow?

You may be one of those that has managed people for years and now wants to let go of the reins. Or indeed you may be wishing to increase your people management responsibilities. Let's look at each scenario.

Increasing your people management responsibility

If it's in your blood, then go for it. Check out new jobs that will initially offer you a larger team than you had previously and include you managing other managers or team leaders. At the interview, make it clear that you have a passion to increase your leadership responsibilities so that you can become more strategic in running your department. Explain that you have an inspirational leadership style including charisma and sharing business vision, and you can strike a balance between managing people firmly and fairly. However, be prepared to back all this up with concrete examples, and don't pretend or you'll look like an idiot.

Decreasing your people management responsibility

Fear not, there is absolutely nothing wrong with diminishing your people management responsibility if you have had enough of it. It isn't about being seen as a failure, but more about being true to yourself, so avoid any self-sabotage. As your Life Bitch, I am giving you full permission to let go of this responsibility and breathe a sigh of relief, my darlings. However, be prepared to explain your way out of it at the interview. Tell the interviewer that, after years of managing people, you have decided you would prefer a role that uses your other capabilities such as analytical skills, customer focus, coaching and development of others, and commercial awareness. If you have only managed people for a short time, then explain that you have decided that having gained people management experience, you now wish to develop a new range of capabilities that you are confident the new role will offer.

Managing people for the first time

If the passion is running high to manage people for the first time, then certainly go for it. Consider the downsides as well as the upsides. Sure you will be able to develop and support people to be their best, but you will also have the challenge of managing their negativity, their sickness and their inability to do a job. Are you willing to be called the bitch from hell and be unpopular at times? Are you capable of making members of staff redundant one day? And do you have the personality to deal with people at all levels in an organisation? If the answer is a resounding 'Yes', then go for it.

Question 4: Where's my confidence level?

Whenever we move on to a new job, it is essential to check out your confidence level. Aiming high is not always good even though some so-called gurus would say so simply because they have read it in a book! Take a confidence check first. If you are currently suffering from a confidence virus, then take some time to get it back to normal as soon as you can by using some of the mind techniques described in Chapter 6. These techniques will increase your confidence and begin to make you feel on top. It is often worth waiting for your confidence to grow, rather than applying for a new job too quickly. Setting your sights too high without the matching level of confidence is a recipe for disaster.

If you are riddled with self-doubt about carrying out the job of your dreams you are fucked so forget it. In my opinion 80 per cent of doing a job well is about confidence and 20 per cent is about your skills, so if the confidence pool is currently shallow build it up first and feel really confident you can do the job well before you apply for it. Otherwise, quite frankly, after a few months you may well get fired and that will make you feel more like a snail in its shell. Confidence isn't just about the job, it is about the culture, the type of organisation you fit. There are still quite a number of so-called macho organisations out there, so if you are not confident that you will fit in with these so-called 'toughies', then steer clear. The last thing you want is an emotional breakdown after a few weeks. As mentioned earlier, align yourself to organisational cultures that fit your values and get a job that fits your personality.

Question 5: What is my gut saying?

Your guts do many things but rather than merely blowing wind they are also responsible for one of the most important aspects of your life – intuition. Over the last ten years in making business decisions, I have always tuned into my gut instincts. At first I thought it was a little crazy to think my gut would tell me what to do, but then I began to realise that by using my gut feeling I made more right decisions than wrong ones. In other words, my intuition became one of my best friends.

Intuition is driven by your subconscious mind. It connects you with your emotions and is in effect an advanced recognition device. Your subconscious mind finds a link between the situation you face and your past experiences, even though you may not recall those past experiences. And even if you can think back to experiences, you will probably find it difficult to recall and use the lessons you learnt from them.

However, the great news is that your unconscious mind still remembers the patterns learnt. What will happen is that your new circumstances – in this case searching for a new job – will be sent a message from your unconscious mind to help you understand which decision is right. In other words, your gut feel is a message of wisdom. The message will usually be expressed as a feeling, a hunch. It will or will not feel right. So, how do you tune into your intuition? Here are a few techniques:

1 Make sure you pay attention to your emotions. One very practical way is to take a good walk or do some exercise. Perhaps go for a stroll and experience nature, and enjoy the calming effect this brings you. Alternatively, practise relaxation, or meditate on your own, and let yourself sink into your own inner world. Imagine that any nervous tension is drifting out of your body as you breathe out. In other words, declutter your mind and then listen to what your inner voice is telling you to do.

2 Write down what naturally comes into your head. Note key facts and feelings that you have during the day. Allow your unconscious mind to let out the information it needs to release. At the end of the day, take a look at what you have written and let the messages guide you in making a career decision. You could also keep an intuition diary, making entries from your dreams, thoughts, and sensations. Review it, and again look at what it is telling you.

3 Drift into a deep state of relaxation and ask your inner mind to speak to you at a conscious level. As you enter a deep relaxed state, often known as the trance state, then ask your unconscious mind to guide you in making your next career move. Your unconscious mind knows everything about you, so be friends with it. It protects you and guides you if you allow it to. Ask it to do so over the next few days. This advice and technique may seem like rubbish to some of you, but believe me, tapping into your intuition and hearing what it says will take you on the right track to the job and career that really is for you.

Question 6: Great expectations?

Finally, have a really good think about what your expectations are with regard to the job you want to grab hold of. You don't want to become a job hopper, so write down all of your expectations, then, when you finally accept a new job, you know that your needs are going to be met. Consider the following questions to take stock of what you really want.

- What salary do I require?
- What kind of responsibilities do I want to take on and let go of?
- What training and development opportunities must I receive?
- Do I want flexible working arrangements? If so, in what way?
- How far would I commute to my next job?
- What role will align itself to my long-term goals?
- What skills do I want to continue to use in my next job?
- What will really motivate and excite me in my next job?
- Do I want to work alone or with a team in my next job?
- What kind of culture do I want to work in?

Being certain about your expectations will help you plan your next move and certainly manage your time better by applying for jobs that meet your needs. If you know exactly where you want to go, and why you want to get there, you will stand much more chance of reaching that dream job.

Now you know what you really, really want from your next job or career move, you are in a great position to put your house in order. By this I mean you can through all the stages of research, planning, honing your skills, writing the perfect tailored survey, preparing for interview and nailing that job aspiration.

Move on from here, take that step. It could be your first job, or it could be you getting out of the rut you've got wedged in and realising that you have much more to offer and gain by changing your job and doing something totally different. Together we can do this, so let's not waste any more time. Let's realise your great expectation.

Real life

Daisy

Daisy, who's now 22, did well at school and got great A Levels, but decided that she wanted to travel around the world and not conform by going to university. She'd had experience of working in a major music venue and liked the vibe that bands and their entourages generated when they came to gigs, but she didn't know which way to go or what she would do.

I got to know her through a mutual friend and offered to help her find some direction in what to do for a career. It wasn't difficult to understand that she was mixed up, but the key was to find out where her true passions were.

I set her a task, to go and prioritise what she wanted from the work that would bring her her daily bread. She came back and told me it needed to inspire her, to get her to think around problems, and also to give her a real thrill; above all, which was typical Daisy, it had to be 'unconventional'. With a little feedback from me, she decided it had to be something in the music industry that got her meeting people and using her skills which were very face-to-face, with the ability to influence people and understand what they want. We decided that she would be great as a music promoter. Easier said than done, I hear you say, but, again with some determination and searching, we found promotion agencies. I helped her to get her CV together and think about how she needed to present herself. The rest was easy because she had a real passion and knowledge for music. She landed a trial position with a music promoter in London within two months.

Jude

Jude, who was 26, had dreamt all her life of qualifying as a nurse and working in an accident and emergency department. She got the degree and then the job, but found that she detested the politics and crap that can get in the way of treating patients. She became bitter and wanted to get out, but felt she didn't have an escape route.

I met her and gave her some advice on listening to her gut feelings about her career and coming up with priorities which could help her escape the wrong decision she'd made in going all out for nursing. The upshot was we decided that she'd quit moaning about the NHS and would be personally determined to try to do something to change it. She was lucky enough to get a consultancy post with a political lobbying group whose top priority is changing the health service. She loves it.

Job Grabber *check list*

- Use your intuition
- Go through the six questions to help you decide
- Assess your level of confidence
- Manage your expectations

Capable of anything?

5

Landing your next job role means ensuring you fit your employer's (or potential employer's) person specification, and a key part of this will be having the necessary capabilities to deliver what they need. Employers will consider four core areas, namely skills, knowledge, attitude and behaviour. This will mean having a good hard look at yourself and identifying the areas where you have shortcomings, as well as knowing, and building on, your key strengths.

It will mean that you need to put in some hard work, face realities and take personal responsibility. It is vital that you confront any areas of weakness and tackle them head on. Never run scared like some bloody chicken that can't pin issues down and deal with them, because you can. Right now I'm going to show you how.

Get yourself fit for the challenge of laying your hands on that new job or promotion with an audit of where you are right now. Follow my six stage process to ensure you'll be the ideal fit for the career step that you have in mind.

The six steps

1 Draft a Strengths, Weaknesses, Opportunities and Threats analysis (SWOT)

Start with a personal analysis of your strengths and weaknesses in relation to the job you want to grab. By identifying your strengths and weaknesses you will have a clear picture of where you are starting from, and you'll know what the opportunities and threats are in getting you to the goal. I would advise you to ask a friend or colleague who knows you well to validate what you have written. It's important that you do this to take off any rose-tinted glasses or illusions you might have about yourself.

Have a look at my example below:

The job to grab:

ADVERTISEMENT SALES MANAGER
IN THE MEDIA AND PUBLISHING SECTOR

Strengths that support the goal
- 👍 *Three years' experience as a sales team leader for a stationery supply business*
- 👍 *Influencing and rapport skills*
- 👍 *Experience of working in a fast-paced environment*
- 👍 *Strong customer service skills*
- 👍 *Leadership skills*
- 👍 *Degree qualified*

Weaknesses that hinder the goal
- 👎 Lack of experience within the media and publishing sector
- 👎 No contacts in the media and publishing sector
- 👎 Little knowledge of how the advertising sector works

Opportunities to overcome weaknesses to achieve the goal
- 👍 Access to online information about the media and publishing sector
- 👍 Make contact with a publisher to gain specific understanding of the industry
- 👍 Attend local networking groups to meet professionals within that sector
- 👍 Tailor CV so that it is aligned to the needs of the media and publishing sector
- 👍 Contact the Institute of Sales and Marketing for advice
- 👍 Contact a senior professional in the media and publishing business and ask for the opportunity to observe what goes on. Ask if they will give you a chance to do some work experience

Threats that could block achieving the goal
- 👎 Being perceived as not having the appropriate experience
- 👎 Self-doubt and lack of personal belief
- 👎 Procrastinating

As you can see in this SWOT analysis, the candidate has clearly identified his weakness as lack of sector experience, but has managed to identify six opportunities to eliminate it. He has also identified the threats that could block achievement.

2 Seek out the necessary experience

- If you consider you don't have the necessary experience for that new job then seek it out
- First identify what specific experience you need to top up on. Perhaps it is a specific skill, such as presentation, or maybe it is more about gaining some specific sector knowledge, or it could be that you currently work in a role where you do not manage people and your dream job requires you to have that experience. You could ask to take on some projects at work that give you the relevant experience, or consider gaining the experience out of work by volunteering to support a charity or community project.
- Remember, people won't hand this kind of work experience to you on a plate so get off your arse and hunt it out.
- If the experience is specific to an organisation you want to join, then be cheeky and just ring them up and ask to spend a couple of days in their organisation. This is especially important for graduates. OK, you may have a degree, but remember you now need to get some real-world experience. A degree is something that many more people can get these days, so don't be over-confident and let your head swell just because you've got a degree.

3 Educate yourself

- A lot of employers won't give a jack shit whether you have a degree or not. On the other hand, it may be in your interest to study for a professional qualification that is aligned to the job you want to get hold of.

- Perhaps you currently work as a personal assistant and have a passion to work in human resources, or you work in credit control and have a determination to move into accountancy. If this is the case then I would strongly recommend you study for the necessary professional qualifications.

- Most professional roles are governed by a professional body, such as the Law Society for solicitors and the Institute of Sales and Marketing for marketing executives. Get on the phone and seek out institutions that deliver the appropriate qualifications.

- Short courses can also be a good choice. For example, if you need to top-up and refresh your legal experience, a short course can often be a good bet.

- If you are in a job and you know you need to retrain, just get on with it. Quit the 'jibber jabber' about going out of your comfort zone. We know that successful people identify what they need to do to improve themselves and just do it.

- Make sure you do some form of personal development or education every year. 'Lifelong learning' is the watchword in the world of work, so don't get left behind and washed up and forgotten like some victim of a shipwreck.

- Winners set themselves learning goals. Get into the habit of setting your own realistic learning goals

- Remember, it is never too early or too late for learning and the options are broad and flexible – you can now learn by distance learning, e-learning, continuing education, mature student places and university postgraduate qualifications. There are no excuses.

4 Build relationships with those who can influence

- Successful people have the ability to build relationships and contacts that last. You should mirror this behaviour.

- Get on the phone and ask for advice and meetings with people who can influence your career. For example, if you are currently working in one department and have your sights set on working in another in your organisation, then call a respected senior manager in the other department and ask to meet for an informal chat. Get on his/her side and create a relationship. Or, if you want to change the organisation you work for, then find out who works there, who is well thought of, and ask to meet them for lunch. But please, no sleeping your way to the top!

- Once you've got your foot in the door with a company you want to be a part of, ask them if you can spend a little time in the department shadowing them, or arrange a meeting with the director or head of the department you want to work in.

- Be sure to show genuine interest in the people who you want to build a relationship with, and show your appreciation. Always email a thank you note to those who support you.

- Never feel guilty about asking others to help you. It shows you are keen, committed and ambitious.

- Business is based on relationships, so never under-estimate how powerful forming them can be. How often have you heard the saying 'It's not what you know but who you know'? There is a lot of mileage in this saying, so my advice is don't waste any bloody time. Get out there and build the relationships.

5 Get a role model

- A great way to build your drive and capability to develop your life through a better job is to model excellence.
- Ask a sports person what he/she did to build competence, and they will tell you that along the way they modelled how their heroes did it.
- Role modelling is a process of observing how an individual does something, then following the same patterns of behaviour yourself. Do make sure you choose the right model to get you where you want to be. It's no good looking at how Sir Alan Sugar got where he is and what makes him a success if you want to become a writer, or mirroring Simon Cowell if your ambition is to head the web development team you are part of.
- Firstly, find someone who you consider behaves in a way that you believe demonstrates excellence. Select them to help close your 'capability gap'. Notice their behaviours and skills. Maybe it is the way they communicate with charisma, or their skills of persuasion, that have got them where they are today. Keep taking mental notes of what they do in as much detail as you can, and then imagine yourself adopting the attitudes and actions that have made them a success. As the days and weeks go by, imagine yourself behaving as they do. Over time your unconscious mind will begin to process and register these new skills or behaviours. The success characteristics and habits will become a natural part of you.

6 Boost your self-belief

- A belief is simply a label you have decided to accept about yourself, and the good news is that self-limiting beliefs can be reversed and made into empowering beliefs.

- Boosting your belief is simple, so let's avoid getting hung up on how difficult it is going to be. As you can imagine, it bores me to tears when people say how hard it's going to be to change their self-belief.

- The thoughts you have about you, your future and your potential are going to play a huge part in whether you grab that new job and are capable of performing it.

- From this moment, you are going to take control of your thoughts and programme them so that the stash of positive thoughts outweighs the negative. Together we'll kick the shit out of the negative thoughts so they can't stand up and be in your mind any more.

- Affirming your positive belief is simple. The thoughts you consistently put in your mind will have a direct effect on your belief in how well you can do the new job and your confidence to grab that new job. The thoughts you need to pick up have to be positive and strong at all times. You should know that the words you say to yourself will produce pictures in your head which in turn trigger emotions that will affect both your physical and mental actions and behaviours.

- In Chapter 6 you will work through a number of techniques that will dramatically boost your self-belief. I am going to condition your mind so that you are a real winner.

Get your head around your skills

Having a clear picture in your mind about the skills and experience you can offer to grab a new job or win a promotion can be tricky. We can all be guilty of overlooking our true skills and the things we have done before that could help clinch the dream job.

You need to assess exactly what you can offer to help you build the perfect CV and to pull out the most relevant skills you have for each job you go for. If you can get your head around this, then you'll understand many of the elements that make you into such a great product.

Don't worry if your head's going into a spin. I've got a great way to pull together a true picture of what you can offer by drafting your own skills audit.

Auditing your skills will help you to take stock of, and recognise, the job skills and behavioural capabilities you have to transfer into new employment. It can also be very useful in identifying where you have a 'skills gap' and prioritising what you need to do to fill any holes.

The skills audit has been designed to help you to identify easily your unique portfolio of strengths, weaknesses, and areas for development within various skills areas.

How to complete this audit

Read the skills area, and place a tick in the column that best suits your ability. Then, in the final column, decide the priority for you in the development of this skill.

The skills area is not an exhaustive list so feel free to add some of your own.

Steve Miller

SKILLS AREA	I CAN DO THIS WELL	OK, BUT I NEED MORE PRACTICE	I CAN'T DO THIS	PRIORITY DEVELOPMENT OF THIS SKILL 1 = very important 2 = quite important 3 = not important
Numerical				
I am capable of making simple calculations				
I can present numerical information accurately				
I can competently use a variety of numerical techniques (e.g. percentages, fractions, decimals)				
I can interpret and present information in graphs and illustrations				
Information Technology				
I am conversant with Microsoft Word				
I am able to use Excel				
I am confident using PowerPoint				
I use email confidently				
Managing Self				
I manage my time well				
I manage pressure so that I do not become stressed				

SKILLS AREA	I CAN DO THIS WELL	OK, BUT I NEED MORE PRACTICE	I CAN'T DO THIS	PRIORITY DEVELOPMENT OF THIS SKILL 1 = very important 2 = quite important 3 = not important
I delegate work to others				
I am able to organise myself				
I have self-belief				
I am emotionally resilient				
I monitor my emotions and act on them appropriately				
Communication Skills				
I demonstrate active listening				
I handle interpersonal conflict well				
I deliver business presentations well				
I communicate assertively in my dealings with others				
I have a professional personal appearance				
I am comfortable with written communication				

Steve Miller

SKILLS AREA	I CAN DO THIS WELL	OK, BUT I NEED MORE PRACTICE	I CAN'T DO THIS	PRIORITY DEVELOPMENT OF THIS SKILL 1 = very important 2 = quite important 3 = not important
Customer Focus				
I am able to use a range of strategies to engage and satisfy customers				
I manage customer complaints competently				
I am able to present ideas to others on how to deliver customer excellence				
I can develop others to support the delivery of customer excellence				
I am able to evaluate how well I deliver customer excellence				
Team Working				
I work well as part of a team				
I demonstrate a positive attitude when working as part of a team				
Managing Others				
I am able to demonstrate effective leadership				
I can provide clear vision to others				

SKILLS AREA	I CAN DO THIS WELL	OK, BUT I NEED MORE PRACTICE	I CAN'T DO THIS	PRIORITY DEVELOPMENT OF THIS SKILL 1 = very important 2 = quite important 3 = not important
I manage the performance of those I lead				
I can motivate the behaviours of others				
I am able to discipline and, if required, dismiss employees				
I can build a team				
Influence and Persuasion				
I offer convincing arguments when getting others to see my point of view				
I use positive body language when influencing others				
I think through the rules of influence before persuading someone to do something				
I am able to avoid becoming defensive when others do not share my point of view				
I can negotiate to achieve a win-win result				

Steve Miller

SKILLS AREA	I CAN DO THIS WELL	OK, BUT I NEED MORE PRACTICE	I CAN'T DO THIS	PRIORITY DEVELOPMENT OF THIS SKILL 1 = very important 2 = quite important 3 = not important
Commercial Awareness				
I understand what it means to be commercially aware				
I am able to describe what is happening in the economy and how this affects business				
I can describe the role I play in building commercial success for companies I work for				
Personal development planning				
I am able to identify my personal goals				
I can identify my strengths and areas for personal development				
I am able to identify opportunities for developing myself e.g. university courses				
I can plan and present a logical plan for my personal development				

Now you have completed the skills audit I recommend that you use it for comparison with the job/person specification for the post you want. Make sure you can tick all the boxes that the job requires and go a step or two further by offering more. With your audit you will have a fuller picture of the skills and attributes you have, and how they can open up the doors to a brilliant job and brilliant future.

Real Life

Tom

As 22-year-old science graduate Tom's only work experience had been as a checkout operator during holidays whilst at university – but surprisingly, given his degree, his career goal was to establish himself in human resource (HR) management.

After he had produced his own analysis of his strengths and weaknesses, the glaring weakness was his obvious lack of real experience.

To overcome the lack of experience Tom decided to cold call a number of human resource departments, but was knocked back 36 times! He'd shown real determination to get a meeting, or advice from an HR department and on the 37th call he got a breakthrough and was invited into an HR department for a meeting with an HR director in an NHS Trust.

He used this excellent opportunity to explain his passion for working in human resources. The HR people he met were so impressed that they offered Tom a paid three-month fixed-term contract. Not only that, but the director who was responsible for taking him on was so bowled over by his work and attitude she offered him a permanent contract after his initial three months.

It only goes to show that good old-fashioned dogged determination pays off. He had a clear vision of the role he wanted, and never gave up on trying to get the first step on the ladder that he needed. His perseverance and positive attitude paid off.

Juliet

Having worked for over 16 years in the finance department of a large manufacturing company, at 48 Juliet felt her skills had gone as far as they could with her employer. She's very well qualified and has professionally recognised accountancy qualifications.

Looking at her skills and ambitions, Juliet decided she wanted to move to work for one of the big four chartered accountants/business advisers. She understood she had plenty of on-the-ground accounts experience and qualifications, but recognised her sector background might hold her back.

To overcome what might have been perceived as a lack of experience in the broader business world, she decided to attend a local 'women in business' group. From her regular meetings she developed a range of relationships, including one with a senior professional at PricewaterhouseCoopers. They met for lunch and she made it clear she was interested in moving into a major professional consultancy.

From this contact she was invited to meet one of the partners in the regional practice who was immediately impressed with Juliet's presence, commitment and style. Two months later she was offered a position as a consultant for the organisation.

David

A 27-year-old sales executive for a software company, David was very happy where he worked and did not want to move on to another organisation. However, he was desperate to get a spot in the company's management team.

With three years' experience behind him and good contacts in his department, including its director, he requested a meeting to go through his ambitions and ideas.

As an example of his drive he offered to part-fund himself to complete a diploma in management studies through a distance learning programme. He also wanted to demonstrate how serious he was to manage a team and asked for opportunities to lead a specific project.

He was given the responsibility to manage a sales project to market software to a large defence company and relished the opportunity. His leadership on this project was second to none and he won the contract.

By taking personal responsibility to educate himself, going out of his way to seek out new responsibilities and nurture business relationships with key decision makers, David was appointed sales manager for a team of 12 within two years. It shows that identifying a skills/experience gap and taking some proactive action to fill it will impress any employer.

It's not easy to look objectively at what you have to offer a potential new employer, or to dig out what can be improved to help you rise in your current job, but the SWOT and skills audit will get you off to a good start. Don't mess around, get SWOTting.

Job Grabber *check list*

- Audit your skills and experience
- Grab more skills and experience if you need them
- Make connections with the right people and get a role model
- Boost your self-belief
- Check you have gone through the skills audit

Get Off Your Arse belief system 6

Have you ever wondered what many millionaires, top sports people and those who extend their life expectancy, even when told they have a few months to live, have in common? It's undoubtedly that they all share the most incredible self-belief; they see, feel and hear a solid faith inside them that guarantees that they have six noughts in their bank balance, get a gold medal around their neck or live years beyond the prognosis of their life-threatening illness.

In this chapter I'm going to show you how to increase your level of self-belief by using the power of thought. Understand right now that if you are serious about it, you will do a combination of these techniques *every* day. There's no room for pussy-footing around and doing bits here and there, you have got to be *totally* committed.

Steve Miller

A warning first. If you suffer with epilepsy or clinical depression please seek advice from your GP before engaging in any of these powerful positive thinking protocols.

What follows is a combination of techniques that will utilise your creative mind and instincts: the powers that we all have if we could be bothered to tap into them. If you have a functioning mind then you already have the power, and I'm sure you have thoughts about yourself, others, life and what may or may not happen in it. I bet you also have thoughts that create so much wonderful pleasure in life! We'll leave those for another book.

What I will do is show you how to steer your thoughts, so that you not only boost the way you perceive yourself, but also the way in which you will inspire the interviewer when you go and grab that new job.

The rules

Before you read on, take note of my three golden rules when doing these techniques:

1 Only do them when it is safe to do so. In other words use your loaf. The last thing you want to be doing is practising one of the techniques when driving or operating machinery.

2 Do them daily, otherwise it may be a case of remaining in that dead-end job. I have no time for people who start but don't finish – lazy fuckers!

3 Do them in a comfortable room, somewhere quiet, and ensure you tell the other half to keep out.

Belief techniques

Here I will outline six positive thinking techniques. Which ones you decide to do is entirely up to you, but you have got to start using them to grab hold of the job opportunities that could be yours.

One isn't better than another, so don't start thinking, 'Shouldn't I be doing the other technique because it could produce better results?' They are all based on clinical applications of hypnosis, proven to get results and are completely safe as long as you stick to my rules.

Try a few of them and I'm sure you will develop your personal favourite. Once you have found your favourite, stick with it and practise it on a daily basis. I will say that the six hot techniques are all aligned to get you to increase your personal capabilities, perform like a star at the interview and improve the way you see yourself. If you think it sounds like bollocks, shut up and just get on with it. I am practical and common-sense driven, but I also know that this works. I have taught this over a number of years, working with people from all walks of life who have tried and tested them with fantastic results.

All of these techniques are better done when you enter a state of relaxation, because you will rest the conscious part of your mind so that your unconscious mind will more readily accept the new suggestions you want to make to it.

Get relaxed first

You need to understand some tips and techniques to get relaxed. I'll now explain how you will relax. First, find a quiet, comfortable room, turn off the phone and make sure you won't be disturbed.

- Sit in a comfortable seat, an armchair is best, and place your feet flat on the floor. Put your hands on your thighs.
- Close your eyes and take six deep breaths slowly.
- Let any thoughts drift through your mind. Let them come and go, avoid fighting any thoughts that may be there.
- Slowly imagine each muscle of your body, starting at the top of your head, melting into a state of relaxation.
- The important thing here is to avoid rushing; this should take you about 15 minutes.
- When, and only when, the muscles of the body have relaxed, calmly begin mentally counting down from ten to one. Try counting out each number on every other out breath and imagine letting go of nervous tension as you breathe out. As you get to number one, picture different muscles melting into a wonderful state of complete relaxation. Now imagine your whole body bathing in a small pool of relaxation.
- You have achieved a perfectly relaxed state and you can now begin to utilise one of the positive thinking techniques.
- Once you have done your positive thinking, count up from one to ten and open your eyes at seven to re-orientate yourself – to coin a phrase 'you're back in the room'.

When you have mastered the relaxation process, read through each of the techniques detailed below and select the one or two that you think will work for you. Simply go with your gut instincts on this and if one of them stands out and it feels right, or a voice in your head shouts 'Yes that's the one', then use it.

1   The Inspiring Interviewee

This is a rollicking technique to boost your interview performance. It has won awards and been showcased extensively in the world's media.

Begin by entering a state of relaxation and then picture seeing a theatre with a curtain covering the stage. You have come to see the production of 'The Inspiring Interview' and, guess what, you are the star of the show. You take your seat and feel a sense of excitement as you are about to see yourself in the production.

See the curtain rise and hear the applause increase in volume. You, as the star, are centre-stage. Picture yourself very clearly and notice what you are wearing, how you hold yourself as you sit in front of the interviewer. Notice how fresh and radiant you are.

You can see the interviewer now as she begins to ask you to tell her about yourself. Notice how you speak clearly and confidently, the tone evenly paced and at a pitch that grabs her attention as she looks at you with curious interest. You're smiling and relaxed, and the natural rapport that continues lets your conversation with the interviewer flow like a gentle stream, a stream of natural conversation.

You notice the questions and how you answer them with confidence, self-respect and a feeling of ever-growing optimism. Allow the real positives of the play to intensify. Note the positive elements and actions that you are seeing, hearing and feeling. Just let this picture of the inspiring interviewee sink deep into your mind.

When you have done so, count mentally up from one to ten, and at the count of seven open your eyes.

Keep practising this and you will be the 'mutt's nuts' when it comes to delivering a fantastic, convincing and job-winning interview.

2 Anchored Beliefs

This has to be one of the simplest techniques for priming and pumping up self-belief. It's about sticking to positive beliefs, facts and outcomes, and not getting dragged down by any negative sentiments; hence I call it 'anchored beliefs'.

Once you have entered a state of relaxation, simply affirm statements of fact about yourself. These may be, for example, 'As I walk into the interview I see and feel a sense of confidence about myself', or 'I hear and feel myself answering questions during the interview confidently and calmly'. Make these kinds of positive statement your mantra and let the unconscious part of your mind bury them in your mind for the situations when you need them. These are statements that will work *for* you rather than *against* you.

You can add to the impact of your mantra by imagining seeing or hearing yourself being part of the mantra. Do always keep it positive: for example, avoid saying things like, 'I will not be nervous at the interview'. Instead change this to, 'I am calm and confident as I enter the interview room'.

See your mantra of you confident in the interview room as you mentally say to yourself that you converse with the interviewer with a feeling of calm confidence.

This is a good technique to start with if you have little or no experience of utilising the technique of positive thinking. When you have finished, and just before you count up from one to ten, tell yourself these new anchored beliefs will be part of you both in the present and the future.

Count up in the normal way and enjoy the new feelings of anchored beliefs.

Now you don't have to suffer the emotional storms that your mind previously experienced when you faced the perceived stress of a job interview situation.

3   Regressed Bests

Enter a deep state of relaxation. For this, the deeper the feeling of relaxation you have the better. Once you have done this, drift back to a time when you felt incredibly good about yourself.

Mentally relive this experience and intensify what you felt back then when you'd really achieved something that made you feel great and confident.

Try to see and hear the experience clearly, as though it was happening to you for real right now. Allow this little film to play in your mind for around 60 seconds.

Enjoy reliving the experience and let your physiology change so that you sit with confident body language in your seat. For example, hold your head high and allow your body to sit up straight. Let yourself think and feel that you are in the zone once again.

Now, feeling that sense of intensified confidence, feeling good about yourself, mentally pick up those feelings and move them into the interview that you have coming up. When you've won the job/promotion you can pick up those feelings again and move them into the new job you have successfully landed so that you perform it brilliantly.

Think of it is as though you are creating a fusion of two experiences, one that has been stored in your subconscious and one that you create using the feelings and emotions of the positive stored memory. Once you have completed the fusion, repeat it three more times before counting up in the normal manner.

We often think of regression being used to allow bad memories to bubble to the surface, but this technique is all about pulling out the useful positive memories that will really help you to get your career going where you want it to go.

4   Bad Habits Binned

Think of your mind being like a swing bin. You can easily throw in negative thoughts, and keep bad memories piling up in it. Over the years you have probably dropped tonnes of what I call the 'demon garbage' into your mind, all those self put downs, telling yourself how shit you are at this and that.

The constant repetition of this 'destructive script' means that you have probably conditioned yourself to create a store of limiting barriers. Sod the barriers, it's time to push them out of the way. Imagine you are in one of those car chase movies and there's a barricade across the road – get your foot down and your arse into gear, eyes fixed forward, because we are going to crash through the mind blocks.

This technique will help you to get rid of this destructive script of yourself by disassociating the bad memories and reintegrating success habits. The success habits will ensure that your mind is in shape to shine at the interview and to go forward and perform the new job brilliantly.

The mental action of binning the bad habits is a creative process that, even if you have had a go, at first seems a bit hippy trippy, but believe me, I don't do bullshit so you had better believe it works.

Sitting in your chair in a relaxed state, imagine a symbol, a sound or even a feeling that represents what holds you back from being 'knock-out' at a job interview. Let that symbol, sound or physical feeling of negativity drift out as you exhale on your breathing and let it go as far as possible into the distance until it disappears altogether, once and for all. Then, from the very point where the negative disappeared, create a symbol, a sound or a feeling of positivity coming towards you as you inhale. Absorb it and let it become a core part of you.

Carry out this routine as many times as it takes to cleanse your subconscious of the demon garbage that has polluted your progress in the workplace.

Having done this, and finishing with the inhalation of a strong positive thought, now see, hear or feel yourself as a dynamic, charged and determined person.

In essence, you are training your brain to understand that in interview situations you are in control, confident and positive. Although this is clearly mind-over-matter stuff, I'm not asking you to bend spoons or turn water into wine. What I need you to do is resolve to dig out the positive abilities and confidence that we all have.

5 Desensitising Anxiety

This is a technique I often use when working with people who come to me and present a phobia. I would say it is a more advanced technique than some of the others we have gone through, but with practice you will quickly get the hang of it. It was invented by a guy called Joseph Wolpe, to help reduce negative psycho-physiological reactions to imagined and real difficult situations, otherwise known as phobic reactions.

In the interview or work situation, you will be aware at a conscious level of how you ought to react to challenges, but it will be your unconscious mind that will have the real influence on how you react and ultimately perform. This is because that part of your mind (also known as your limbic system) contains memories and emotions, along with automatic functions such as heartbeat and breathing patterns, that come into play according to the situation. This area of the mind governs the way you react, so we need to learn how to stop it running away with itself. In other words, your unconscious is pre-programmed using your life experience and imagination and will control what happens in the here and now.

To illustrate what I'm saying, just imagine you had an experience with an interviewer who was a complete arrogant fucker which resulted in you feeling anxious. It may very well be that, the next time you have an interview with someone else, that memory could determine how you behave: in this example, feeling like shit on the interviewer's shoe.

Forget that and put the crap in the bin because you can change these unhelpful conditioned responses by reprogramming the unconscious part of your mind by a process called systematic desensitisation. It involves you imagining a number of conditioned responses to the interview, or starting the new job, and merging this 'dream' with relaxation and confidence.

Why does it work? Simply because it's not possible to feel both anxiety and relaxation at the same time. Feeling relaxed is much more conducive to performing well, as you will then be able to answer questions clearly, have natural body language and build better rapport. All of these factors will help you to progress your career successfully and grasp positive change.

Blending relaxation with the anxiety-provoking situation will help reduce the anxiety at the interview. If you decide to use this technique, you need to be aware that you will be bringing out the same anxieties that have been damaging in the past, so only attempt it if you are prepared for this. *If you do suffer from severe anxiety, then go and see your doctor first, as you will probably need to work up to this technique.*

How to desensitise

To desensitise you must construct a scale known as a Standard Units of Disturbance Scale (SUDS). The SUDS is a progressive scale from 0 to 100.

For example:

0 . . . 10 . . . 20 . . . 30 . . . 40 . . . 50 . . . 60 . . . 70 . . . 80 . . . 90 . . . 100

Now think of the specific elements of a job interview that can trigger your unhelpful anxious reaction and plot them on your scale between 0 (which represents a state of no anxiety or disturbance) to 100 (which represents the state of most anxiety or disturbance). For example, driving to the interview may have a SUD of 40. Entering the interview room may have a SUD of 80. Answering questions may have a SUD of 95!

Once you have plotted the SUD scale, you will easily be able to pinpoint the different components that have made the prospect of a job interview so challenging. You may in fact feel you are great at interviews, but we all have some room for improvement in most of the things we do, so do this and improve your SUD scores towards the 0 mark.

In order to desensitise each SUD, follow the seven steps below:

a Enter a state of calm and in your mind see, feel and hear a favourite place of relaxation. It could be the beach, your favourite armchair or a Jacuzzi.

b Picture t2he least disturbing scene from your scale.

c As you picture the scene, notice the accompanying anxiety it triggers.

d Now let your mind go blank.

e Go back to your favourite place of relaxation.

f Now bring back to mind your anxiety-provoking situation. You will notice the feeling of anxiety is beginning to drop as you melt the relaxation into it.

g Continue repeating the above process until you can think of your disturbing scene with comfort, easing the SUD down to a low score or a perfect 0.

This technique needs perseverance, but it is incredibly helpful in improving your ability to limit your anxiety and boost your calm and confident approach to the interview situation. Eventually, you will be able to approach in a far more relaxed state the memory of a situation that triggers anxiety. Once you have conquered the least disturbing scene, move on to work on the next one up the scale and so on.

Your mind will begin to associate the different events with a state of calm, rather than the current unhealthy anxious state. The real key here, and to understand about this technique, is that while you are thinking about your relaxing place, how great your skills are, your in-depth knowledge of the organisation you want to join etc., there's no way you can think about being nervous because you are going to be late for your interview, or you'll freeze when they ask you questions. Remember, the negatives can't be there at the same time as the positives.

6 Tough Talk

As I'm sure you'll have gathered 'tough talk' is one of my personal favourites, and you can use it whether you're relaxed or not.

If you are one of life's whingers, then it's time to give yourself a kick up the arse. There are too many blamers and victims in life, so perhaps it is time to take responsibility for once. It's time to tell yourself to 'shut up, cut the whining and just fucking do it'.

Tell yourself you have reached a turning point. Long gone are the days of moaning that the job is too dull, or you dread going to work because of the boss. In this technique, you accept that you talk like a loser but at the same time make a contract with yourself to act, change and move forward. Perhaps you mentally accept that a moaner's talk will go out of the window from this moment on, or have a realisation that you have been a silly little shit who puts more thought and energy into moaning than anything else. Now you agree it is time to move forward positively.

Real Life

Harry

Harry, a 22-year-old graduate, had no previous work experience at all. His mum and dad had funded university and his lifestyle expenses (there were plenty). You might say he'd had a silver spoon in his mouth for far too long.

With everything put on a plate for him, he didn't really understand what it was like to get out there and take hold of what he most needed – his first job. Inside his mind, Harry was incredibly anxious about attending job interviews, so, after a string of dismal failures which knocked his confidence even more, he decided to do something about it.

Harry started to practise positive thinking using 'The Inspiring Interview' and 'Anchored Beliefs' techniques.

Within six months of graduating, Harry was successful at securing a place on a management training scheme with a blue chip company.

Susie

At 52 Susie hadn't worked for 11 years, having focused on her family and bringing up her three children.

Her previous experience was grounded years before, working as a middle manager for a retail organisation. Susie had a massive dilemma because she needed to get back to work to help support the family, but was absolutely terrified at the prospect of sitting in front of an interview panel. She'd even been offered interviews, but had freaked out and couldn't go.

Whilst she had been confident in her previous role, she reported a dent in confidence but couldn't explain why. The anxiety was so intense that even when posting her CV she would end up in tears.

I worked with Susie over three weeks, using the Desensitisation technique I have explained. The process helped Susie reduce tensions to get the confidence to apply for a management role and then attend an assessment centre selection day. Even though she failed on the first attempt, Susie managed to secure her dream job at the second attempt.

Simon

Simon is a 34-year-old management consultant who's been around the block once or twice. If there was an award for 'moaner of the year' Simon would win it hands down. I would have been more than happy to put the crown on his head on more than one occasion.

He may have had the brains, but his common sense was non-existent. To be honest, as a client, he irritated the pants off me from the word go. He was unhappy in his job, criticised his director at every opportunity and was clueless about what to do about it. At this point I yelled ACT!

What Simon needed was some no-bullshit tough talk, and he received just that. I told him to get his act together, cut the criticism of others and look to himself for answers on moving forward.

We started this process with him in front of a mirror and critically looking at himself. I mean really looking in a mirror, and also writing down what he felt his capabilities and weaknesses were, and his ambitions. By analysing his current state, we were then able to look at moving forward. He muzzled his mouth and agreed to monitor his damaging-self talk, build a professional CV and apply for roles that he was attracted to.

Once Simon realised that the whinging about his situation would never get him anywhere, he learnt that he needed to develop his own resolve to change his circumstances and plan a way out of the environment that he couldn't develop in.

Having kicked out the moans and yakking, Simon eventually acted on his own, registered with an executive head hunter and grabbed his next senior appointment three months after we had met.

Boosting your self-belief is the lynch-pin in being successful in grabbing the job or career that you really want. You may have settled for second best and written yourself off time and again, but believe me, if you can believe in yourself you can do anything and get what you want. Start practising the belief techniques and get that self-confidence and determination going.

Job Grabber *check list*

- ○ *Talk with your GP if you've ever suffered from, or do suffer from, depression or epilepsy*
- ○ Practise the techniques daily
- ○ Find your favourite technique
- ○ Make sure you've bolstered your self-confidence

Mission ambition

A mbition brings out the best in us and it can also bring out the worst, but ambition in the context of grabbing a new job or building a career is all about having the motivation to improve your current situation. It is about your ability to do well, and truly spank your own arse and get it to move up into top gear so you make the most of your career prospects.

If you are a warbling moaner, then it is time to turn up the volume of your ambition, drown out the moans, and channel the positive energy so that you make the most of you and your talents.

To be honest, I cannot understand people who have no ambition – and to me ambition isn't just about money and materialism. It can be just as much about getting a new job that drives you, interests and stimulates you. If you are one of those people who have plodded from job to job, then it is time to rev up your ambition.

Being ambitious and translating that into career success is now very much at the heart of our popular culture, and it's this that shows up the good and bad elements of ambition that I touched upon earlier. Programmes like *Master Chef* highlight what ambitious people can achieve through preparation, improvement, skill, self-belief and determination; while something like *The Apprentice* shows that some people sacrifice their dignity and values in order to achieve their short-term aim of a moment of fame. Let's be honest, it's not about getting to work with Sir Alan Sugar or Donald Trump, it's about being on the telly! The ambition I want from you is the *Master Chef* kind.

It's never too . . .

It is never too early or too late to be ambitious. Take a guy I came into contact with on my business travels: Alex Wolf, a 22-year-old call-centre agent, who is already in talks with a number of publishers for his book, *The Cull of the Innocents*. This guy's ambition impressed me. He explained that he was determined to be a successful writer when he left school and it was always in his heart and soul. Even though he was bullied at school, this guy fought back and never let go of his ambition. He explained he had always been an outsider, but never lost sight of his goal. His dream to write the book was for a solid reason – to prove to himself that he could. The novel fired his creativity and at the age of 21 he was successful in finding an agent. His ambitions continue, and he is now writing his sequel. Part of his ambition is to give something back to those who have shown him support and love along the way. The inspiration for the book is based on his opposition to seal culling in Canada and this passionate belief continues to fuel his ambition.

This is what I want from you: be inspired and driven to go for your ideal job or promotion, not because others tell you it's the right thing to do, or because you can't think of anything else to do, but because you *want* it.

Leave the comfort zone

There's another guy I know, Michael, a 52-year-old city worker who left the big world of banking to channel his ambition to set up his own consultancy firm. This now turns over a million pounds a year. Michael decided that his experience was well placed to help him set up the business. He left the comfort zone of his well-paid post, put all his savings into the consultancy and, as he explains, 'worked my bloody socks off day in day out to make the business grow and succeed'.

Ambition is also about enjoying the risk associated with change. Remember, no risk, no glory. If you want fresh challenges, an increase in material wealth and to do something you really want to do, then risks must sometimes be taken.

How to increase your level of ambition

First, let's get one thing straight: being ambitious is your responsibility and no one else's. It's not mine, your parents', your friends', your partner's, your kids'. It is *yours*!

Now is the time to get ambition into your head. There isn't an injection you can give yourself, but there is a mind-set change. And don't start coming out with the shit that losers always use which is, 'Oh, but I just find it hard to motivate myself.' That bollocks is a thing of the past, OK!

Right, now we have got that out of the way, we will continue. I am going to give you the six Get Off Your Arse actions to help increase your ambition. Just get on and follow them. It's time to just fucking do it rather than contemplate your navel and hope that things are going to change themselves for the better.

1   Identify what turns you on and off

Get yourself a piece of A4 paper and write a heading: 'Hot passions'. By passions I'm not talking about the sexy stuff, so cool down and focus.

Brainstorm all the things you love, then write them under the headings. These can include the things you enjoy doing in life as well as in work. For example, one passion may be entertaining friends, and another may be sharing ideas with lots of people. Alternatively, it may be that your passions include working with complex data and travelling to new places around the world.

This is the start of your own self-assessment, and an opportunity to rediscover what triggers your ambitions. Let's face it, over the years you will probably have changed and so will your ambitions. You may currently be working for a fast-paced commercial organisation, but your heart-felt passion could be to work for a not-for-profit organisation. Your passion may be for caring for vulnerable people, rather than currently working with tough business suits. If you know in your heart that you should be doing something different because it will nourish your soul, as well as your bank account, then start grabbing and do it. It might sound glib, but you've only got one shot at this life so be true to yourself.

2   Research new careers

Now you have got to grips with what will get you turned on and motivated to get out of bed, it's time to research what careers meet your passions. If you feel nervous, just get over it and remember those who succeed take a risk or two on their journey. This is the start of an exciting new chapter in your life, not the dull, samey, safe existence you've had up to today.

Search online for the career opportunities that you are now beginning to identify will meet your hot passions. There is plenty of job info, career descriptions and people talking about what you want to do online, so go and dig it out. Have a look at your hot passions and then search for jobs and careers that your common sense says will meet them. For example, if you enjoy organising events and socialising with lots of people, then perhaps event management is something you could look for. Or maybe you enjoy working on your own, problem solving and using your analytical talents. If that's the case, then you could consider becoming a data analyst. It could be that your passion is for a particular cause and you enjoy helping people. You could then search for information on what it takes to become a counsellor or a charity support worker.

3   Set the goals now

By now you have researched the job/s that fit your passions and you have your ideal job in sight and in mind. Go with the instinctive choice that fits your passions, feels right and ignites your desire. Make a decision *now* and stick to it.

Having selected your ideal job, it is time to set the goal. This goal needs to be really **SMART**. In other words:

Specific – the job that you want

Measurable – the practical actions you will take to achieve that job

Agreed – you feel 100 per cent this job is right for you

Realistic – you have the ability with training and education to do this job

Time bound – the date by which all the actions will be complete so you are in a position to apply for the new job. Also, the date by which you will be appointed into the new job

Real Life

Sonia

Sonia was 32 and an experienced PA, but she felt she was bored and had a frustration that she wasn't being true to her talents. She had begun to wake up in the morning with diminishing motivation levels. She said she had passions for supporting the public, physical activity and solving problems. After some extensive background research, she identified that her ideal career change was to become a police officer.

I sat down with her and she completed the following **SMART** goal plan:

Specific – to become a police officer

Measurable – receive career pack by 1 March; return application by 31 March; source a personal trainer by 5 March; lose half stone in weight by 31 March; source support with interview skills by 10 April

Agreed – my heart and mind are committed to this career change

Realistic – with support on physical fitness, I will have the ability to be selected

Time bound – appointed 1 September

Sonia joined the police force she'd dreamt of – and not only that: she showed promise so quickly that she was selected for fast-track career acceleration and has joined the swelling ranks of senior female police officers. Go girl!

David

As a senior recruitment consultant, 33-year-old David enjoyed the people aspect of the role, but felt the sales element was not his bag. His passion was for people and customers, and he especially enjoyed leading project teams. David identified that his ideal career goal was to attain a position working for a leading call-centre operation

David's **SMART** goal plan showed:

Specific — attain the role of call-centre team manager

Measurable — tailor CV to call centre team manager posts by 30 November; contact UK call centres to advise of interest and forward CV by 30 January; research preferred call-centre organisations by 30 January; set up and practise mock interviews by 10 February; enrol on a diploma in management studies with the Open University by 28 February

Agreed — I am totally committed to and focused on this career route

Realistic — I have transferable skills

Time bound — to be appointed by 30 March

I can say that David was one of those people prepared to take the plunge for their dream, and he went on to nail a senior role with a highly regarded call-centre group in India.

Jain

Jain came to see me as a 26-year-old human resources manager. Her ambition was to become an HR Director within the next few years. Jain felt it was time to get some real focus and boost her own self-belief, as she had taken some personal as well as professional knocks over recent years. During her first session we sat down and developed her **SMART** goal plan:

Specific — to attain the role of Senior Human Resources Director in the NHS

Measurable — to have completed an MBA by 30 October; to have upgraded membership of the Chartered Institute of Personnel and Development by 1 June; to have redesigned her CV by 30 June; to have contacted head hunters with a new CV by 30 July

Agreed — yes, completely passionate and focused and will complete the DIP process (see below)

Realistic — I have four years' experience working at a senior level and have covered the director's role in the absence of my own

boss. I also have a strong academic background and strategic competencies to fulfil the role, in addition to sector experience
Time bound — To be appointed by 1 December

Jain is one of those bright stars who shine and give off that positive vibe to all who meet her. It's no surprise that she was given the job of leading the HR function for one of the country's larger PCTs just after her 27th birthday. She also tells me that the decision to bite the bullet and go for her dream brought back the confidence that she thought she'd lost for good.

You can see from the SMART goal setting examples above that those things can happen quickly if you want them to, but goals can also be long term. Ambitious people see a connection between what they are doing right now and where they want to be in the future. Begin thinking each day when you get up to do your current job, or whatever your day brings, about how it connects to your future goals. Avoid the daily moan about going to work, going to college or looking after the family. Instead, look to the future and link what's happening now to positive steps that will make you successful. Moaning will simply magnify your dead-end rut, so cut it out right now!

4 Get into the zone

You have got to become really excited about the opportunities available to you. I am often shocked to see and hear people do nothing but moan and groan about what life offers, failing to notice there's a big world out there and that we can, if we put the effort in, reach new heights.

Getting into the zone means that you become excited, enthused, and determined to put the effort into grabbing that new job. It has to be better than sex! Yes, *better* than sex. Dream big, aim high and kick out from your life the negative drainers that hold you back. Bin those who want to put self-doubt in your mind.

Practise the following DIP process daily, so that your dream becomes stored deeply in your unconscious mind. Over time your mind will become more and more focused to achieve that new job, so much so that it becomes as natural as driving a car. DIP means:

D – Define the vision. See, hear and feel yourself as though you are already in the job. Notice what you are wearing, how it feels to have the title of that job on your business card, and pay attention to any sounds such as colleagues talking to you in the new job.

I – Identify the parts. This means, in your mind's eye, identify all the really positive things you did to achieve the job. This may include taking a specialist qualification, inspiring the interviewer and networking with those who can help influence your career goals.

P – Play the movie. Having defined your vision and identified the parts, then play the whole lot. Sit in your chair, relaxed and comfortable, and enjoy the movie. Your own epic! Start with the first part and then the second and so on. Play them all and build up to the final vision. Then I want you to go a step further. Adjust your body language so that it matches the movie in your mind. Sit up straight, and use relaxed open gestures. Act as if you are the Queen Bee of the movie. Enjoy, my starlets!

5 Self-esteem – build and build again

'Learning to love you' may not sound very Get Off Your Arse, but believe me it is. You have possibly knocked yourself down so often and put so much crap into your head for far too long, that it has made you rein in your own ambitions. You've found it nearly impossible to be ambitious, especially if you have no belief in yourself, so you are going to need to do the daily belief boosting techniques outlined in Chapter 6.

As you build your self-belief, what will follow is a series of doors being opened. Your increase in self-esteem will mean you feel naturally steered towards what once seemed only a dream. As your ambition accelerates, your competitiveness will be healthy – but be careful that you don't piss people off along the way by being unhealthily competitive à la *The Apprentice*. Build a *daily* self-esteem ritual by using positive thoughts and statements about yourself. Doing a few one-off exercises will not turn your lack of self-esteem around and build you into the winner you can be: you need to do a belief boosting technique every single day. If you can't be arsed, then stay where you are and don't move forward.

As your self-esteem builds higher so does your emotional resilience. Quitting will never be part of your language again. You have your eye firmly placed on the next job you want to grab, and you never get thrown off course, because you value you and know you deserve it. Thomas Edison's most outstanding quality was that he never quit. It wasn't that he was so much smarter than everybody else; it was just that he never quit. It took something like 10,000 failures to make the light bulb.

6   Stay clear of office politics

Most organisations and offices have their share of office politics. Personality bitching, resource bitching and power bitching are all forms of office politics. I dread to think how much productivity is lost as a result of people at all levels standing around bitching about everyone else except themselves! It's just misdirected and wasted energy; it's hot, smelly air.

You are well advised to steer clear of all of this. If people try and drag you in, be diplomatic and don't take sides. Instead spend time advancing your own business projects and focusing on your end goal. Forget all these idiots who simply want to enjoy the drama of backstabbing others. You don't want to be labelled as someone who can't be trusted, so keep politics at arm's length. Getting into office politics will add nothing to your ambition plan.

Instead, steer your energy into positive work relationships where they matter. Develop a rapport with all your colleagues, especially those who can help you as you progress. Yes, be seen to be accommodating, flexible, hard working and go with the programme as long as you believe. Egos are fragile, so stroke the ones that need it at the top. If others around you talk of you as an arse licker, then it is their fault they don't know how to do it as well as you do. Remember it isn't always skills that determine promotions. It is your reputation; it is you as a brand.

Your mission now, and I know you've chosen it, is to ratchet up your ambition and direct this positive energy right where we need it to go. You'll fly up the promotion ladder and inspire at interview. I want you to aim high with newly found, or newly invigorated, ambition, and don't take no for an answer.

Job Grabber *check list*

- Understand ambition and what your ambitions are
- Remember, it's never too early or too late to start being ambitious
- Follow the actions to increase your ambition
- Use SMART goal planning
- Practise the DIP technique
- Aim high, but be comfortable with it

Big fish or little fish?

With small companies making up a larger percentage of the economy, many more job opportunities lie within companies employing less than 100 people. The question you have to ask yourself is: Do I want to be a big fish in a small pond, or would I prefer to join a larger organisation and be a small fish that could grow into a prize catch?

As someone considering a new job, you will find there is always a conflict between moving to a large company with a big brand and all the bells and whistles that larger organisations can offer, or a small/medium company where you might start in a senior role and get involved in the business's broader future.

I will help sort out this decision in your mind. We'll get cracking by taking a look at the pros and cons of each option, breaking down what you could expect to happen in a smaller organisation and then a big one.

Steve Miller

The big fish

Pros

1 Joining a small company means you are more likely to go in as a big fish, or become one more quickly. Your experience and skills will be valued and needed, and you can create an impression quickly.

2 It is more likely you will learn more, as there are fewer policies and procedures and everyone should know how to work on everything. Moving from one department to another is less difficult, and so gaining comprehensive experience is a lot easier.

3 Because smaller businesses tend to ask you to do more in terms of different skill areas, their job opportunities tend to be more challenging. By getting about and doing more, your face is going to be more visible to the directors. It is less likely you will be 'just a number' because your contact and intimacy with colleagues in the professional sense is far greater.

4 Smaller businesses and organisations are often more free of politics, and conflicts tend to be identified and sorted out quickly.

5 You get to see a lot more of the business as a big fish in a small pond because you will get to know more of the people and be given wider responsibilities. Even the MD may sit next to you and work with you, helping you out at times.

6 The company owner and senior staff are more likely to be on-site, so you can learn from their entrepreneurship.

7 Because of their closer relationships and tighter teams, I have found that there tends to be a more fun attitude surrounding work in smaller organisations.

8 Employees who work in a smaller company, especially if it is a start-up, are very enthusiastic and expect to see similar passion. They are very driven and want the company to succeed. This makes life exciting and you will learn so much about how to run a business and grow it.

9 In a smaller organisation there is no room for a lazy arse. They get found out very quickly. The business can't and won't carry these people, so you can expect all employees to have to pull their weight.

10 The great benefit of working for a smaller business is that you will probably get an impressive job title – you're the big fish! You may join as the accountant but in fact be titled Finance Director. It looks good on the CV, so bear that in mind.

11 The smaller organisation will generally also provide a quicker route to the very top. If you are very ambitious and want to have director status soon, then being in a small company will probably be the better choice. If you play the game well, the MD will in all likelihood create the position for you.

Cons

1 Working at a small company can be a lot of work. With resources so limited, you may be asked to work 12–16 hours a day to get your product or service out there. Believe me, if you have a '9–5' mentality and join a start-up company, then it's very likely the welcome mat will be pulled from under your feet. If you are not willing to be flexible then forget it. You'll need a 'can do, will do' attitude that sees you doing jobs that aren't in the job description and volunteering to help in different areas when the need arises.

2 You can normally expect a lower salary at a smaller business than you'd get at bigger ones because resources are limited. So, if a high salary is what you value most, then perhaps go to the bigger companies.

3 There are few mentors available within smaller businesses, so there is more pressure on you as they won't often have the time to facilitate your development.

4 There are fewer training and development opportunities available at smaller companies. Budgets are limited and the first thing to be cut in times of weak order books will be the training budget.

5 If you work for a small company, it will be far more difficult to be spotted when you want to step up to join larger concerns. If you apply for another job and have worked for Virgin, you will most definitely be identified. On the other hand, does working for Furnace and Sons Ltd really have the same impact?

6 In the future, larger employers may perceive you as being inexperienced if you have not tasted the big bad world of corporate life.

7 Transferability to another department will be more restricted in a smaller company compared with the large business that can often offer you a complete change of job as well as location if you so wish.

8 If you are not up to the job in a small company, then this will be spotted very quickly, probably within just a few weeks, and you are likely to be fired. The large organisation has more

time to train and coach you, but the smaller company cannot afford to carry poor performers.

9 A posh job title may be easy to obtain in the small business, but, when it comes to moving, be prepared to struggle to attain similar status if you want to jump to the big organisation. You may have to take a step down in terms of perceived status. Consider that this move may skew your CV from high status to lower status – from 'Financial Director' at the small engineering company to 'Assistant Financial Controller' at the multi-national engineering group.

10 If you don't get on with the owner of the small business, you are well and truly stuffed. Personality clashes are dealt with rapidly in a small business and the owner will always win.

The little fish

Pros

1 Joining a big company will most likely mean access to bigger salaries, and pay increases are likely to come sooner rather than later. Development opportunities are certainly going to be more plentiful.

2 If the larger company you choose to work for has a strong brand, then your CV is more likely to be sexier in the sense that future employers will instantly recognise where you are from.

3 With a bigger company, and as a smaller fish, it is more likely you won't be under the performance spotlight, so failure to perform well in the role is less likely to result in rapid dismissal.

4 In a big company, you're assured of a steady pay cheque. You don't need to hold your breath every quarter to see if the company is going to enter a redundancy process.

5 Part of the excitement of working in a big company is that you will be surrounded by a heap of talented people. You will have the opportunity to interact with experienced leaders and soak up their knowledge.

6 Of course when you get promoted in a big company there's always someone at a level higher than you to learn from. You are able to take hold of their experience as they will have been round the block a few times with plenty of insights and advice to offer you.

7 Being able to master the politics is often seen as a plus in the bigger company. Promotion in this case can follow quickly as you know which people and groups to be close to.

8 The big organisation usually offers structured training opportunities, therefore professional as well as personal development is a dead cert.

9 Thee large company will appraise you and take a more structured approach to your career. There are more likely to be opportunities for secondments and to work in other parts of the business.

10 Your role in a large organisation is far more likely to be perceived as having higher status than if the same title exists in the smaller company. The challenge is becoming the big fish in the large pond!

Cons

1 Politics oh politics! The organisation will have them and they can get so frustrating and a bit messy at times. This can affect daily life in the office as you wonder what you can and cannot say and who you need to stroke and who you need to scold. This can be so very draining!

2 Whilst a large salary can follow sooner in a big business, often the downside can be that financial returns from the large companies that decide to go public are often not as enticing compared with those that have decided to stay private.

3 It is fine being employed with a big company whose brand is established, but if the company goes tits up you will be part of that brand and that reputation.

4 The big business may talk the talk, but does it deliver? The bigger company often has more meetings and jaw-jawing time to develop slogans and promises that may be well written but not acted on or delivered.

5 Working in the larger company, it is easier for people to do little and never be found out. Working next to lazy shits who aren't managed may frustrate the hell out of you.

6 The big companies often love rumours, most of which are not true, and before you know it hundreds of people are aware of them. They could be about you.

7 The need for you to play the game is higher in the big company. You will have far more egos to stroke and rules to follow.

8 It can get comfortable working in a large organisation. The salary is easy money and your face may fit for now. When the day comes that your face is no longer popular and, believe me, that will happen, and you have clocked up 15 years with the big company, then it may be difficult to move on. You may be typecast by the big company you've worked for and the role you had.

9 Cliques are more likely at the larger business. Are you certain you will be accepted by the ones you need to be part of? If you join the big company only to be ostracised, you may have some serious emotional issues. It does happen, believe me, as I have met several people who have faced this and been emotionally and mentally bankrupted!

10 You may need to attend lots of functions with the big company. The annual Christmas party, the annual awards dinner, the networking events, the boss's birthday party, customer events. This may be your bag, but if it's not, then be very aware.

11 Within the hierarchy and command structure of a larger organisation or business, you could get frustrated at the way decisions are made. This could be by committee and take ages, or it might be a fairly autocratic process, with power in the hands of one or two people who do as they please. Either way you may not like it.

So, there are definitely good points and bad points to working as either a big or little fish in a small or large company. Which is better for you will come down to your personal preference and the risks as you see them. Success can come as both the little or the big fish, so the choice is yours.

Do remember that the little fish can grow to be the king fish in a major business, but it's going to be down to your talent and skills, hard work and probably a little luck. For those of you who want to be the big fish with a small company, then do remember that you will take on a lot quickly, and hence you may outgrow the pond soon and then find it difficult to get into more open water with a larger company.

What I want you to do is have a look at the pros and cons of each. Get a piece of paper and write down the merits and de-merits that most stand out for you. Then rank them out of ten. The higher the score the more important it is. Look at your total scores and then subtract the cons from the pros for both the little and the big fish. The highest score will indicate which fish you really should be.

Job Grabber *check list*

- Weigh up the pros and cons for big and small companies
- Do your personality and skills set suit a big or small organisation?
- Where will your ambitions be able to come to fruition?
- Write down the merits of a big and a small company from your perspective and score each out of ten

Relocation expectations

9

An important factor in making a decision about a career change, or starting for the first time, can be moving to find the right job. It can be a difficult decision to take, but for thousands of job-hungry people it is a reality every year.

Moving to a new town can have its perks, but there can be downfalls so you have to get your head around it. Relocation is among the most stressful events that can happen to an individual person, or of course a family group.

Relocation involves a number of variables being weighed up and carefully considered, including financial, personal and emotional issues. These variables can contribute to stress in varying degrees, depending on your personal circumstances. Taking a new job somewhere else can often contribute to breakdowns in relationships and marriages, and to losing contact with people who have been friends for a long time. This is a big decision that can't be treated lightly.

One of the most difficult situations to consider is a scenario where the main breadwinner in a family has been offered a 'dream job' with promotion, better salary and greater opportunities. For many, the opportunity of taking on that dream job is too tempting to refuse.

I am all for relocation if your ambitions are being fulfilled, and it's pretty easy if you are single, but if a partner and children are involved, it's time to work out between you what's most important for you all.

If you are a couple with no kids, and the dream job is your dream career that's been out of reach so far, and he or she is a dead head then move on. In fact, moving away will help get the loser out of your head and hopefully they won't linger around, knowing that you are going to be miles away.

I recently met a charming young woman on a flight to Edinburgh and she worked in marketing. I found our conversation so inspiring as I listened to her explaining how she was relocating to Switzerland, having ditched the hubby. The kids were now grown up, established and self-sufficient – it wasn't that she couldn't care less about them, but was quite the reverse: she loved her children, but knew they now had the life experience to cope on their own. Good for her! What a role model of excellence she is.

Moving away can bring a better job and really great prospects from a better job market. If you are struggling to find a job in your area, then moving to a different part of the country – or even to a different country like the lady mentioned above – does make sense. Career opportunities can sometimes be limited to certain regions of the country because of economic change, so moving away will bring you greater confidence to get the job you want, and what's more it could well offer greater opportunity for advancement.

It's not just about the job, though, is it? It is about your growth, about you developing as a person; it's about you! You will create new relationships, gain new experiences and perhaps meet the man or woman of your dreams.

Decisions, decisions – how to decide

Let's consider some of the questions you need to ask yourself. In my time I have helped many people to decide whether to accept a job or not. It can be a big decision, but then again, you can't piss around for ever.

To aid the decision take a look at the questions below.

How will it affect your family?

The decision may impact on your kids, if you have them. They will probably have to move schools and make new friends. If you have a partner, they may not want to leave their friends and/or job. And of course if you have elderly parents to consider, then you will need to make arrangements. It may have an effect on other members of your family, but come on! This is *your* life. If you have to go home at weekends for a few months after relocating, to sort out family affairs, the move, etc., it is worth considering if your new employer will offer flexibility so you leave early on a Friday.

If you are close to your loved one, and have kids who will be uprooted, and they'll all be desperately unhappy, then your relationships could well be put in jeopardy, so forget it and stay where you are. Otherwise it will be tears at dawn every five minutes, and that will irritate the arse off your new work colleagues. If, on the other hand, the loved one is a rat, then fuck 'em and bugger off!

How will it affect your friends?

It's going to be a no-brainer for some of you because, if they are friends you can count on, they will support your decision and continue to be good friends. However, you may be so tight with your buddies that you don't want to do anything without their 100 per cent blessing. If you move away from them, then yes, it's going to have a big impact on how you get along, but don't forget: if the bonds are strong they will not be broken.

Do you give a shit how a move will impact on others?

Considering the above, and if you have a heart, then yes, you will care deeply. However, there are ice maidens out there, and guys who would sell their soul for a few dollars more, and if that's you, you will drop everything to move on for your own reasons.

The other point to consider is, if you are doing the whole job move and relocation deal for self-preservation, then maybe you need to admit that No.1 does come first and foremost. Sometimes you really have to cut out the shit and do it for you.

Where are you going to live and will you get some assistance?

It will, of course, depend on the position you attain, but always negotiate assistance if possible. The new employer may offer help in finding a new place to live, and, especially for senior management roles, may well cough up and pay some expenses.

A good company will usually help by paying for a house-hunting trip, or even pay for temporary living accommodation, including hotels. However, I must offer a word of caution as these expenses will be viewed as a taxable benefit, so don't think Santa has come early!

What about schools for the kids?

If the family is going with you, then check out the local schools. How do they fare in comparison with the current school adorable Amy and ranting Ryan attend? Are they going to offer them as good a level of education and support as their current school?

Get talking to parents, check out the school itself, and have a look at its results. If they don't compare and meet what you want, all is not lost. You may have to move a little further out of town. They're your kids, so you owe it to them to look after their future in this way.

How much is your heart in it?

First of all, be aware that things in life do go tits up, so have a contingency plan. When you leave your employer, try to keep the door open as best you can. If that's difficult and you really think the new job isn't going to work out, then don't go. In fact, before committing to a new job, ask yourself how much your heart is really in it, on a scale of 1 to 100, where 100 means you are 100 per cent positive. If you register 90 moving up to 100, then get on with it. Anything less, then I would forget it.

Jacquie, a colleague of mine, worked as a display advertising manager for a local newspaper, and before that she had run her own business. She enjoyed a stimulating challenge. After she'd worked as a display manager for eight years, she decided it was time to move on, but her concern was leaving her 80-year-old mother who needed her support.

Jacquie was head-hunted for a regional publishing director's role which would be based in the Midlands, nearly 150 miles away. However, it was a dream job, and one she was eager to fulfil. Jacquie took a proactive approach as her heart was 100 per cent in taking the new job. She had a few niggles, but took care of them by deciding she would manage her time and see her mum at weekends. She arranged additional care, and reassured her mum that all would be fine. Jacquie then hunted for accommodation and was supported by her new employer to relocate. She hasn't looked back since. What really mattered was that Jacquie was self-motivated and committed to making it work.

Are you moving for a fatter pay cheque?

Be cautious if the answer to this is 'Yes'. Relocation also involves a lot of expense. Make sure you research the location. Is it safe? Let's face it, knife crime is rife at the moment so safety is a key consideration. You may have to move to an expensive area, away from where you will work. Check out the commute as you won't want to get to work knackered each day. And finally, what is the cost of living in the area? If it is a bit pricey, then you may have to have a change of heart, given that your disposable income will shrink. My advice is to go and spend a week there and check out all the small details. Also consider that there might be a cultural adjustment, for example, if you have lived with open fields and mountains for years, a sudden move to the city may come as a shock.

Is it all in writing?

Before you hand in your notice, put the house up for sale and start packing, get everything in writing. This should include your contract of employment, and confirmation that the organisation will pay relocation expenses.

It really is dangerous to take everything for granted, so talk to your new employer and ask for written confirmation via post or email. The last thing you want is no current job, no home and no job to go to.

For some people relocating is part and parcel of their career and life. You could be in the armed forces or working for a large organisation that expects its senior people to move on to new positions and departments on a reasonably regular basis. That's OK if you are used to it, and that's what you want.

But, for most of us, relocating is a challenge where we have to overcome emotional and physical ties and we need to make the right decision, otherwise things can go wrong for everyone concerned. If other people are being dragged into the equation, then you need to weigh up carefully all the considerations we have gone through.

Real Life

Jeanette

At 24, Jeanette had set up home near Bath with her boyfriend and started a career in textile design. The two had got their feet firmly under the table and seemed set to stay put, but, as we know, life has a funny habit of changing things for us when we least expect it. In this case, Jeanette was head-hunted by a fashion house in Milan to come and work for them. It happened via a contact who'd been one of Jeanette's lecturers in the past.

The job offer really threw the cat amongst the pigeons. Of course she wanted the job, but her boyfriend wasn't too keen to see her go without him.

Jeanette knew the Milan job was the opportunity of a lifetime, but she loved her partner and pleaded with him to give up his job in the building trade and come with her. Sadly, he wasn't for moving, and Jeanette had to give him the heave ho and go for the job. I'm pleased to report that she's now leading a design team and has found herself an Italian stallion.

Georgia

When she was in her early thirties, with a couple of young children, Georgia was married to a guy who was an engineer. He was offered a job to go and help set up some new exploration facilities in China, and wanted to take the job because it would mean his salary doubling and give him a real career-boosting opportunity.

However, Georgia had packed in her career as a successful dancer to have a family with her partner, and was not going to see him go away for most of the year, leaving her stuck with the kids on her own.

They are a switched-on couple who talk things through before making any snap decisions and judgements. They decided to reach a compromise which was that once the children were a bit older they would then take up an opportunity for her husband to work overseas, but not now. At the later date, the whole family would go, and treat it as an opportunity for them all.

Job Grabber check list

- Consider all the variables
- Ask yourself the relocation questions
- Get confirmation in writing of your job offer, relocation package etc.
- Have you carefully weighed up the decision?

Could going solo work for you?

For more and more people the thought of being your own boss and becoming self-employed is a desirable option and often a dream. Let's make no bones about it though, it takes real balls to go down this route and take on the various risks that you might encounter. But the rewards can be brilliant, from earning more money to having more time and freedom to do just what you want.

You may be sick to the back teeth of working for people who couldn't organise a piss-up in a brewery, so is that what's spurring you to go it alone? Or you may be one of those who have been made redundant and want to invest their time and money in a business that they have always dreamt of.

As an entrepreneur I myself shout from the roof tops about the numerous benefits of going self-employed. Your money is yours, no one to report to except your customers, holidays when you want to take them, and the satisfaction of seeing your enterprise flourish thanks to your own effort and ideas. But hang on, is it really that good? I can honestly say I have never worked so hard since running my own company. The hours are longer, weekends are no longer for chilling out and having fun, and the stress can be incredible.

So, you need to think carefully if you are going to go it alone with the dream of becoming the next Richard Branson. But, if your heart and mind are set on building a business for yourself and you are willing to put in the hard work, then why not? Just be warned again, it's not all a bed of roses.

You're going to need the guts to take risks, and the drive to get through the grind of daily activities to grow, expand and, most importantly, satisfy your customers. Now, if your conviction is still there to become self-employed, let's take you on the journey of making your business a success.

Step 1: Build the brand

So you have a business idea and you've got your heart set on turning it into a business reality. It may sound obvious, but you need to come up with a name that will capture the attention of your target market, one that will tell them what makes you different and what you do: nothing too long, ideally it needs to be one or two words. Think for a moment about some of the well-known brands – Virgin, Auto Trader, Yellow Pages, BMW, and Barclays. Think of your name as a label which gives the customer an idea of what your business is about and what it stands for. You will also need to think about a brand image for the name which may involve the design of a logo, development of a strap line etc.

To promote your brand and develop your business from scratch it goes without saying that you will need to spend your money wisely. Yes, advertising can work if carefully thought out, planned and placed, but advertising will not always bring instant results. What it can do, over a period of weeks, is inform and motivate customers to take action. You can also consider a raft of other integrated marketing tactics, from an emailer to delivering a public relations campaign, to explain your brand, your offer and what's in it for customers.

If you are going to do the above, negotiate the terms carefully and understand that you will have to commit to a marketing campaign that will take several months and absorb your hard-earned cash. But, before appointing an agency, think carefully about the hooks of your brand and why customers and the media would want to pick up on it. Marketing your business effectively is one of the crucial keys to success in the first few years, so invest, but invest wisely.

Step 2: Set your business objectives

So the brand is in place and now it is time to set out your core business objectives. Setting business objectives is essential, and certainly the bank will want sight of them if you need to apply for a business loan. Your business objectives simply set out what you will achieve and by when. They may be short term, usually over 12 months, or they may be longer term, normally up to three years.

It's all very well having business objectives, but you need to identify the actions you are going to take to achieve them. Every year thousands of wannabe entrepreneurs talk about 'what' they want to do, or are going to do, but fail to get off their arse and do it. Tactical actions are the 'making it happen' part of your business plan. Under each objective you list the actions that will be taken to achieve them. All these actions must be **SMART**. Let's take a look at a couple of examples.

Robert

After working for his employer for 15 years, Robert set himself up as a self-employed training consultant. He started his business on 2 January. For the first 12 months he identified his business objectives as follows:

1 To have 15 substantial clients by 30 June
2 To have an annual turnover of £200,000 in the first year
3 To have maintained a cost base of 20% of sales revenue by year end
4 To have attained editorial coverage in a leading-edge training journal by 30 May
5 To have appointed four associates by 30 June

Robert's timeline to achieve the objectives:

Objective 1

- Begin cold calling 30 prospects per day from 3 January
- Design a website with search optimisation by 1 February
- Conduct a telemarketing campaign for the months of March, April and May

Objective 2

- To deliver 12 training days per month from 1 April
- To provide an incentive for clients booking for the second half of the year
- To commence an online advertising campaign from 1 February

Objective 3

- To negotiate preferred rates with suppliers by 1 February
- To downsize car engine size by 1 March
- To work from home for the first year

Objective 4

- To have appointed a PR agent by 30 January
- To have prepared editorial ideas and angles with PR assistance by 28 February
- To have contacted by telephone editors of national HR and training journals by 30 April

Objective 5

- To have placed an online advertisement with recruitment website by 1 April
- To have conducted an assessment centre for associate applicants by 15 May
- To have appointed four training associates by 30 June

Laura

Laura resigned her position as an editor of a respected publication to set up her own glossy women's magazine on 1 June. Her business objectives for the first year were to:

1 Have advertising revenues of £325,000 by year end
2 Have the pagination of her glossy magazine up to 80 pages by 1 February
3 Have a total circulation of 20,000 by 1 March
4 Have built an advertising customer base of 150 by the year end
5 Have implemented a regional marketing campaign by 30 June

Laura's timeline to achieve the objectives:

Objective 1

- Appoint two telesales/field sales advertising professionals by 30 June to increase advertising revenue
- Have an introductory advertising scale for new businesses June–Sept
- Ensure all promotional material, website and online promotion is in place by 1 June start-up

Objective 2

- Appoint 12 editorial contributors for the magazine by 1 June
- Ensure a 60–40 split between editorial and advertising

- Recruit a full-time journalist by 1 September to develop new editorial strands

Objective 3

- Carry out monthly promotions of the magazine in June, September and November
- Develop a mail-out list for magazine subscribers by 2 January
- Identify 50 leading hotels, boutiques, bars and bistros to carry the magazine by 1 July

Objective 4

- Develop a professional media pack for new customers by 1 July
- Design and implement a loyalty scheme for customers by 1 November
- Hold six hospitality functions for potential new customers in September, October, November, February, March and April

Objective 5

- Appoint a marketing consultant for the months of April and May prior to the official business launch, to develop material for the marketing campaign
- Hold a business meeting with former colleague who is a marketing director mid-May for advice on the proposed marketing plan
- Present the marketing plan to the team end of May

Step 3: Get the resources sorted

Once you have your clear direction sorted it is time to think about, and put down, all the information and resources needed for your business. When you have identified these, put a timeline by each of them. Consider, for example, the IT resources your business will require; staffing; office space; stationery; transport etc.

You will need the basics such as business cards, letter heads and, ideally, a website before the official launch of your business. I can't stress enough how important it is to get the infrastructure of your business in place before you officially launch.

Getting the information and resources sorted will help you look more professional and fit for business. Imagine launching a business and a customer requests further details to which you reply 'Sorry, sir, we are in the process of putting them together.' Not good. You will look amateur and it is unlikely a new customer will trust you. Think of it like building a house. Would you really buy it without knowing it has strong foundations? I guess not.

Building your resources often means you need to borrow money. Borrowing money is always a last resort, but if you need to do it then make an appointment with the business banker at your local branch. They will want to hear initially about your business idea, so take along your business objectives and tactical actions in the form of a business plan if you already have one. If you don't have a business plan, then your business bank manager will ask you to draft one following the bank's specific guidelines. When you attend your meeting, dress smartly and present yourself as someone who can be trusted with the bank's money and not as some scruffy arse who's more likely to rob the bank. Remember, it's not only the brand of your business you are selling, but also the brand that is you!

Step 4: Serve your customers well

It isn't all about swamping them with freebies at Christmas, although it's good to at least send a card. Customer excellence is about three core elements:

i *Deliver what you promise*

False promises mean your business is doomed. Equally bad is a promise that is half delivered. Honesty is the best policy, so if you are going to go it alone please bear this advice in mind at all times. It doesn't take long for the message to spread that you are not to be trusted and don't deliver. So many people out there operate contrary to what the trade description laws require – that is, they fail to deliver on their service promise or guarantee. Some people in business are out and out crooks and can't be trusted. Don't be one of them.

ii *Provide immediate solutions to solve customer concerns*

How many times do we complain, only to be greeted by a Rottweiler barking at us at the end of the phone, or end up face-to-face with someone prepared to go into battle with us? If only these novices knew that when a customer complains there are three simple steps to follow. Firstly, listen without rudely interrupting; secondly, empathise by showing that you understand their issue; and thirdly, negotiate and agree a solution. Customers become irate normally because they are stressed. They want solutions. So focus your mind on solution rather than fighting them.

iii *Nurture the relationship and become a business partner*

As an entrepreneur I know only too well the importance of nurturing business relationships. It is vital you get to know your decision makers as people as well as customers. You can never do enough to help your customers, so think well and truly outside that bloody box. Gosh, how I hate that cliché, but it is so true. Helping out your customers, no matter how small their need, will nurture your relationship so that you become their business partner rather than just one of their suppliers. If they are a small business and the owner is about to have a child, take an interest; if they are thinking of taking a holiday to the Maldives and you have been there before, take over your photographs for them to look at; if they want a Labrador puppy, help them find one. In other words become part of *their* family.

Step 5: Manage your costs

So, you are about to embark on one of your dreams. Putting your business plan together ensures that you forecast your costs for the first year. It is common practice for a business not to make a profit for its first three trading years, so don't get too disheartened if the projected profit and loss doesn't initially look too healthy.

Think through your costs thoroughly. Yes, it may look as though times are going to be hard, but that's business unless you are one of life's silver-spoon-in-the gob brigade and mummy and daddy are going to help you out.

The bank will want to see that you have thought through your projected costs, so do this thoroughly. And if possible talk to your own potential suppliers and negotiate hard on price. Remember not to accept the first price they offer. Go at least 40 per cent lower than what they offer and eventually you will meet somewhere in the middle.

As you run your business, avoid becoming a 'showy' entrepreneur, unless you can really afford it. You don't need a flash car; you can take a week in a 3-star hotel in Spain, rather than a 5-star luxury break in Bermuda; and you can get great clothes at bargain prices at TKMaxx and the local supermarket, rather than the designer ranges in the city boutiques. Let me remind you that working solo isn't about immediate luxury. Be under no illusions – it is about hard graft and cutting back when you start out.

Step 6: Consistent hard work

Hard work is the seed of success. Work hard and the rewards will follow. I know this because I've done it. Gone are the days when you think twice about going into work because you have a cold. Here are the days when there isn't a real weekend; the week will not end at 5 p.m. on the dot on a Friday any more. I mean it when I say don't be surprised, especially in the first few years, that you work seven days a week and long hours.

Plot out the consistent activities you will do daily, weekly and monthly to build your business. This may include daily cold calling, weekly advertising and monthly customer visits. Build up a list of these activities that will contribute to the end goal, that of being a business that enjoys double digit profit growth each year. This will ensure your focus is never broken. Successful entrepreneurs never take their eye off that end goal, so plan these activities out.

So, if you ain't willing to get up at 6 a.m. most mornings, work until 7 p.m. most evenings, ditch the 'leisure' weekends, say goodbye to the designer clothes, holidays and accessories for a few years, then forget going solo.

Step 7: Turn the ignition

So is it going to stay a dream, or are you ready for it? Are you going to be decisive and go for it, or are you going to be like one of the sheep and just stand in the field, dreaming about what's on the other side of the wall? If it's not in your blood, if your hunch isn't to get on with it, then don't do it. If, on the other hand, you are revved up at the prospect of launching your own business and are raring to go with a clear vision, then it's time to map it all out.

One of the biggest motivators for people who do go it alone and start their own business is knowing that they have control of their own future and stand or fall on the back of their own decisions. It's interesting to think that most of the major brands we take for granted, from Marks & Spencer to Stagecoach, started from that initial spark of an idea, something small that was driven by vision, hard work and determination.

The satisfaction and rewards from starting your own business can be great; from the personal sense of achievement to being able to earn more money, I love it. The money side can be a lot more than being a 'wage slave' for someone else who takes most of the cream while you sweat to earn a salary that may take years to build into a good wage. Once you have built a successful business, don't forget the freedom that it will bring into your life: working more flexible hours and perhaps getting involved in other projects and fresh ventures. It can be very exciting.

If you firmly believe there is a market for your product, or service, then begin following my steps above. Identify the brand, draw up your objectives and tactical actions, and think through the resources you will need, think through how you will thrill your customers, control your costs and say a resounding '*Yes*' to hard work.

If that is the case, forget the fear and get on with it. Good luck!

Job Grabber *check list*

- Have you got the balls to do it?
- Follow the Get Off Your Arse steps to planning and building a business
- Plan realistic objectives against a timeline
- Get together the resources you will need
- Get on and do it!

The graduate – getting the first job

So the nights of boozing and partying in the students' union are over. The degree is claimed and it's time to think about getting that first job. You need money. It is time to put the degree to use and show employers that not only do you have a piece of paper, but you also have character and the personal skills and abilities that make you a hot proposition.

Whilst being a great achievement, a degree is not a guaranteed ticket into employment, so lose any delusions that you are about to lead the team and be the cream of the crop. The university life and lectures are largely removed from what will now begin to dawn on you is the real world. People will expect you to perform, think for yourself, be on time for work/appointments etc, and to contribute from your skills and intelligence. Don't expect to plonk yourself in front of a computer screen and surf the net on your employer's time, keeping your Facebook page up-to-date. They might let you do that at lunch time if you are lucky.

You've probably gathered I'm not a huge fan of the university system. In fact, I have no time for university lecturers who have been academically institutionalised from the age of dot, and who are hardly ever exposed to life outside this closed world. They rarely have much practical experience to back up their teaching, and I would fire most of them tomorrow. They are stuck in the world of education and should be forced to leave the lecture hall regularly and do some time in real life. And as for the bearded lefties who spout on about social injustices, I would fire them all. Well, that's my own lecture over. Now let's get down to business.

Which path?

For a start, it is highly unlikely you will have one career during your lifetime. Serial careers have become the norm, which I have to say makes things far more exciting. As life unfolds, you may take different career paths as your values change and different experiences come your way. So before you choose, consider that it's likely to change a few times.

Before you rush into a career have a good think about your skills, what type of job is going to push your buttons, and also get a grip on your limitations. For example, if you value ambition, long hours and beating targets, then maybe consider the sales career route. On the other hand, if you rate highly fairness, people and their contribution and equality, then maybe consider working in human resources (HR). Avoid going down a career path because others think you should; forget the fact that your old man was in the army and that's what he wants you to do. Be true to yourself, not others!

Match your skills with the opportunities out there and take account of other factors that affect your job decision, such as personal debt, family dependency and mobility. Spend plenty of time on this process – and you've probably got plenty on your hands – to make sure you have thoroughly audited your skills and can make a clear choice on which path to take.

What employers need

Employers often report the lack of 'soft' skills from graduates. By soft skills they mean things like intuition, verbal skills and motivation. These may not seem as important as your 'BA Hons in Politics', but, believe me, if your soft skills are weak, then you will struggle to land the job you want and progress up the ladder.

When I used to run assessment centres for graduates, I was often disappointed at their lack of common sense, communication skills, teamwork and leadership. We all have these skills to lesser and greater degrees and they can be developed, but many of our graduates score poorly. A graduate may well have a first class degree, but could easily demonstrate sub-standard communication skills. It was rare for me to meet a first class degree graduate who had first class communication skills. Don't get me wrong, they do exist, but are as rare as a lottery winner.

So, what are the skills and behaviours that employers really want to see from you? It's not your ability to drink 15 pints of beer and tuck away a couple of kebabs afterwards! Take a look at the following checklist and that will give you a clear idea of what potential employers often look for from their graduate candidates:

Graduate skills checklist

Communication and interpersonal skills – your ability to converse with others clearly and concisely. But it goes one stage further. The ability for you to develop rapport and manage interpersonal conflict, as well as adapting your individual communication with others.

Leadership – your ability to create followers through your strength of personality linked with common-sense strategies to encourage others to share your vision. Demonstrating behaviours such as assertive communication, passion, empathy and encouragement to others.

Initiative – thinking through and using your common sense to seize appropriate opportunities to achieve the best result, rather than standing back looking like a complete dildo. And of course acting on your initiative, rather than testing theories and scenarios until the cows come home.

Motivation – showing that you are motivated to achieve, and so motivated that they respect you for it. Demonstrate your self-motivation by taking pride in your appearance, your ideas, and your vision. Using non-verbal and verbal communication that indicates self-motivation, rather than looking like a cocky, lazy little sod.

Teamwork – your ability to demonstrate that you listen to others in a team setting, to encourage others, to disagree assertively rather than aggressively as well as having your own opinions. And finally, of course, showing that you have the team's interests at heart, rather than your own. This is very important in establishing you as an effective team player.

So do you measure up? Of course you do! Think about it. During your degree course you will have increased your capability in each of the five areas outlined above. You will have delivered presentations, held and perhaps chaired group assignments, worked as part of a team either in a sport or tutorial group setting, and I would hope you would have needed to be self-motivated to set study time, attain top grades and achieve personal goals. Before you attend an interview, list as many examples as you can of how you demonstrated the competencies outlined above during your time at university. You will be surprised how many you can think of.

Inspire at the interview

You will of course research the employer prior to attending the interview. Only a fool will make the interview the first contact they have had with the company. Learn something new, rather than stale news. Check their website, visit them at a careers fair, or give them a call for a pre-interview chat. Simply explain that you will be attending an interview and that you want to ensure you are fully prepared. Shyness must go out of the door. If the employer is open to the public then go in and talk to the staff as well as key managers. Learn at least three key things about the company. All of this will help you become comfortable on the day of the interview or assessment centre. I was always impressed with graduates who had done their preparation, because it demonstrated initiative, ambition, communication skills and commitment. So get off your arse and do it.

You will be given the opportunity to ask questions at the interview so think of some beforehand. Good questions may include asking

'What has happened to previous graduates who have joined the organisation?' and 'How is the graduate programme structured?'

Here are a few others:

- What opportunities are there to progress with the organisation?
- What planned changes, if any, are there for the organisation?
- How can I make a real impression in the first 12 months of my employment?
- What do you expect that my main responsibilities will be in the first 12 months?

As a graduate it will impress the interviewer if you have constructive questions to ask. It should form part of a statement of your own passion and commitment to do a good job.

If your degree included a placement, then make certain you emphasise this. It's OK if you have a good degree, but seriously, how often are employers really interested in what class it was? Talking about any work experience you have will definitely support your application. You may even receive a higher starting salary, as the employer is more likely to perceive you as an asset. If you didn't have a placement, then discuss other experience from your time at university. Maybe you had a summer job? Even if it was stacking shelves in the supermarket or waiting on tables, it is still valuable experience, especially when it comes to the soft skills we talked about earlier. The secret is to link your experience as well as your degree to the questions being asked by the interviewer.

Finally, a piece of advice that was given to me when I graduated: tell a good story. When you are asked a question by the interviewer, do your best to elaborate on your answer with solid experience from your time as a student. For example, if the interviewer says, 'Tell me what you consider demonstrates fantastic customer service' rather than replying 'Being aware the customer is always right', expand your answer by saying, for example, 'When I was a student I worked as a waitress and I found fantastic customer service included making sure I listened to the customer, met the needs of the customer and always asked them if I could do anything else for them. I think this approach is vital in any customer-facing organisation.' This answer will show you are not only a bright academic, but also someone who has their feet firmly planted in the real world. In other words, you will not look naïve and appear as if you are in cloud cuckoo land.

Graduate job-hunting checklist

- Start now by making a list of your chosen employers.
- Make sure your job choice aligns to your values.
- When you are invited for interview, be certain that you know three key things about the organisation.
- List examples of how you have demonstrated the competencies expected from graduates.
- Contact your chosen employer and, if possible, have a pre-interview discussion or visit.
- Inspire at the interview by asking constructive questions, and reinforce your own answers with real examples of your own experience.

Real Life

Jon

Jon was a 23-year-old geography graduate with a first class honours degree in Human Geography. His ambition was to find a job where he could apply elements of his academic ability and experience. He loved the parts of his degree which taught him about the connections and impacts that people have in their physical environments.

He'd also gained some valuable workplace experience as a student working for a local taxi company. While with the taxi firm, he developed and harnessed excellent communication and organisation skills which helped the business retain customers and grow revenues.

With the degree in his pocket, Jon was determined to work in a forward-thinking professional environment. Prior to his job search and interviews, he identified how the combination of his academic and practical experience would make him a good fit into a consultancy organisation.

During an interview for the type of job he wanted, he was able to answer questions confidently and to tie in the experience he'd had in helping to build up the taxi company's business.

It wasn't long before Jon was appointed as a consultant for a regeneration agency in the South East. At the same time, Jon enrolled on a Masters degree and went on to achieve a distinction.

He's now a senior consultant and is a great example of how being highly intelligent and academic can combine with soft skills to make a very attractive package as a job candidate.

Louise

Louise, a 26-year-old graduate, achieved a good degree in social sciences, but quickly acknowledged that a social science degree was not top of the list for very many employers. She decided she wanted to embark on a career in financial services with a large organisation.

In her last year at college, Louise had called the HR department of a large insurance company near her university and asked if she could undertake a summer-long work placement with them in their marketing team. She was fortunate to be offered a placement and picked up some great work experience.

In other holidays Louise had worked with an events agency in a promotional team dealing with the public. This helped to sharpen her communication skills so much that she relished the chance to go to interviews. The experience gained at the events agency was like gold dust and you should all hunt this kind of placement out. Don't get snotty because you might not get paid anything, or just your expenses, because employers are really doing you a favour by offering a work placement.

When she graduated, Louise rehearsed how she would bring her experience into interview conversations. It only took two interviews for her to be recruited as a graduate marketing assistant within an international general insurance company.

Louise had used her initiative, developed good teamwork skills at university, and was someone who could really tell a great story of getting off her arse and gaining valuable experience to achieve her career goal.

Hannah

Hannah, 23 years old, achieved an upper second class degree in English and really wanted to carve out a career in journalism.

While at university, she had been involved in the university debating society, and had agreed to do minutes of the meetings. In addition she volunteered to be her course representative at staff/student liaison meetings.

Hannah spent some time investigating the various routes into becoming a journalist and decided that she wanted to work in newspapers. Following her graduation, she immediately enrolled in a full-time NCTJ print journalism qualification at Cardiff.

Hannah was determined to seek a trainee post with a regional newspaper in Yorkshire. She was offered an interview and was able to answer questions theoretically, but also with plenty of practical examples.

She had prepared constructive questions to ask at the interview, and had focused her mind on self-belief that she was as good as any candidate, if not better, in this competitive market. Bolstering this kind of self-belief at the right time gave Hannah a real edge and you too can easily do it. (Flick back to Chapter 6 if you need a self-belief injection.)

Taking the postgraduate course really paid off, not only through work placements, but in teaching her basic journalism skills which she was able to demonstrate at the interview. She was appointed as a trainee journalist, and you can't blame her for celebrating. After all, there had been 120 applicants!

The supply of degree courses has expanded massively in recent years, but for many employers this has led to a slide in the quality of graduates and in the qualities that they can bring into a business, or organisation.

My advice is straightforward; while doing your degree think about what career you want to start in and make yourself stand out from the others by getting work experience in the real world. It's often that experience that will give you the edge over other graduate candidates you compete with.

Pull out all the stops and get as much real-world job experience as possible, and don't think that if you have worked in a local store during your holidays that this won't count, because it will. Make damned sure you try to find some work experience or placement that will match your career aspirations. Many organisations, in a range of sectors, will offer graduate work experience placements as a way of getting in touch with quality graduates that they can recruit. Even if you don't get a firm job after a placement, the experience on your CV will glow.

Job Grabber *check list*

- Think about your skills, character and ambitions – match them to opportunities
- Brush up on your 'soft skills'
- Prepare for interviews
- Follow the graduate job-hunting check list
- Think about choosing a degree that will align with a career that you may go for
- Get real-world job experience wherever and whenever you can

The age of experience

I
t's great we are all living longer, and that means we have a big crop of mature talent in the workforce. If you are getting on a bit, things have got much better in terms of being able to work for longer; the opportunities are there and employers can't discriminate against you because you are mature.

The age discrimination employment law came into force in 2006, so by now employers should have got the message that they can't overlook people who want to work for them, just because they are older. The law now provides protection against age discrimination in employment, training and adult education for people of all ages.

There are companies like B&Q that have had a great attitude towards employing older workers for some time, and more and more companies are now at last seeing the benefits in employing the over 50s. I smiled while reading about Sidney Prior, who was 77 when his second career began as a customer adviser at a B&Q garden centre in Wimbledon. Good for Sidney!

As our culture and social attitudes move forward, being over 50 no longer means you are a fossil preparing to put the rug over your knees. The Office of National Statistics says Britain's workforce will expand by about two million people, to 32 million, over the next 15 years as people live longer and work longer. The number of workers aged 65 and over is expected to grow by around 200,000.

In fact, it is regularly being argued that 50 is the new 40 and that 'life starts here'. Being on the scrap heap at 50 is complete bollocks, and anyone who tells you different is talking utter crap. Older people are now bolder people who are using their better health and fitness to remain active in leisure and work. They are doing everything from extreme skydiving to starting up businesses. The future is very sunny indeed for the over 50s.

A good example of how things have progressed is a friend of mine who worked as a self-employed fishmonger for 30 years, then, at the age of 51, decided on a career change and became a store manager for a leading retailer. Three years later he was promoted to area manager. Now, at the age of 55, he is one of the top area managers in the company. He is one of thousands who have changed career at 'nifty fifty' so, if you were losing sight of turning your working life around, you can start seeing it again.

A survey conducted by the Manpower employment consultancy found that half of UK employers are ready to take on older workers to meet the growing skills shortage. The survey of 2,122 UK companies and 1,085 workers revealed that 52 per cent of companies wanted to employ staff beyond the age of 65, but, 81 per cent of staff questioned said they would not want to continue working into their late 60s. Good news on both sides I guess, as there will be jobs for those that want them.

By 2030, according to the British Occupational Health Research Foundation, half of the UK population will be aged over 50. What's more, HR consultancy Aon Consulting recently estimated that the number of workers aged between 65 and 70 will treble to three million by 2017. My goodness, it gets better. Who said you would be over the hill, no good and wrinkly at 50-plus?

The result of the trend for more workers who are over 50 is that more and more organisations are taking a proactive approach when it comes to training and developing the more mature employee. For instance, HSBC Bank now runs online academies, which allow older employees to build their own personal development programme. Through a self-assessment questionnaire, older employees are able to find out where they are in the organisation and then match this against the skills of a position they would like to aim for. How proactive is that!

The leading outsourced call-centre operation, beCogent, operates a similar policy. Their proactive stance on developing employees, irrespective of age, includes an in-house training academy which provides an opportunity for mature workers to develop their management skills, confidence and personal skills such as time management and assertiveness. Employers are definitely waking up to the new age, and life is really starting to begin for many at 50.

Now there's a point to be made for those of you who have worked your socks off and reached your planned retirement age. We've talked about all the opportunities for carrying on working and contributing, but what if you don't want to? Well, *your* job is going to be retirement and enjoying it to the full because you've earned it!

Change now – it's never too late

Employers have had to change any ageist practices as a result of employment regulations, so forget putting your age on your CV. In this day and age it is irrelevant. The changing attitudes and employer flexibility have seen a steady growth in employment agencies looking for mature candidates. So can change be achieved? Of course it can, if you want it.

I have six actions to help you get the job you want as a mature job applicant. You will have to put the work in, so be prepared to roll your sleeves up.

Action 1: Update your skills and qualifications

Job related qualifications are essential in the modern world, so research what specific qualifications you need to train for. For example, if you have been a retail manager for the last 20 years, it would be advisable to achieve the professional qualifications awarded by the Chartered Institute of Personnel and Development. Or perhaps you are an experienced administration manager whose ambition is to train to be an accountant. If that's the case then call the Association of Chartered Certified Accountants or the Chartered Institute of Management Accountants, otherwise known as CIMA, for advice. Not only do they welcome people over 50 on their programmes, but they provide testimonial examples of the mature population entering the profession.

Whatever the change, it is likely you will need to update your skills and qualifications, so get on with it now. Surf the net and check out who you need to call. Contact the sources that will give you access to the skills update that you are looking for. While doing this research, you may also be pleasantly surprised to find that there are sources of grants and funding that will help you to go on courses and pick up the qualifications that you need. There are no real barriers to learning and further development any more, so no excuses.

Action 2: Talk to specialist employment agencies

As the demand for the mature and experienced worker has increased, so has the need for specialist employment agencies representing this sector. That said, don't deny general employment agencies the opportunity to see your CV. Try the Wise Owls employment agency who offer comprehensive support to mature job seekers. Or there is the Wrinklies organisation. Grab a meeting with them. If you are in your mature years and single you never know, maybe you can do a bit of speed dating while you are there.

Action 3: Make the most of your experience

Think through the skill sets you have and recognise the experiences that you have had. List the top six experiences that you can bring to the career change or new job. It really surprises me that people of all ages, but especially those getting on a bit, skate over the experiences that they have had in life and often dismiss things like travelling, looking after relatives, trying a career as a writer etc. as insignificant, things that they shouldn't mention or talk about. That's cobblers. Share your life and work experiences via your CV and at interview.

Mentally rehearse how you will describe your experiences and how they can contribute to your job application and career aspirations. Try and combine this valuable experience with how you have developed as a person. For example, you may have developed professional management skills over the years, but, hand in hand with this, on the personal side you now understand that in life it is important to recognise that people are very different and that when it comes to leading people it is different strokes for different folks.

Play on the obvious strengths and advantages that you have as a mature candidate. For example, in the interview emphasise that you bring steadiness and reliability as a result of your experience, and that you still retain the level of ambition you had when you were 25. If you are clocking up your late 50s, then let the interviewer know that you are inspired not retired.

If it's the case that you want a complete career change, then identify the specific experiences you have had that align closely to the needs of the newly desired career. At the same time ensure you are getting stuck into any applicable professional qualifications.

Action 4: Think of older as better

You are what you think you are, so be sure to reframe any negative thoughts you might have when it comes to your age. Age isn't an anchor that should drag you down, it's a kite flying high that is taking your life to new heights and making life freer all the time.

Being older is better in so many respects. Older often means more freedom, financial stability, fewer mistakes, oh and of course better sex. Oh yes, the technique definitely gets better with age, my sweets. There are so many examples of people who, through their own beliefs and attitude, never allowed age to get in the way of change. Take Anneka Rice, the former host of the TV show *Challenge Anneka*, who, at the age of 50, after tackling 'impossible missions' such as building an orphanage in 48 hours, left the world of TV to study at the Chelsea College of Art. What an inspiration – and she looks bloody amazing!

People in their 50s are often more motivated and bring work and life experiences that can be transferred into other areas. And don't forget, the world needs you now more than ever! Demographically we are well in the shit if we don't look after our so-called oldies because there won't be enough people with knowledge and experience to do what's needed to keep things going – the population is getting older and families are getting smaller. All a wonderful recipe for being proud to be 50!

So, if you have any thoughts, or people are telling you, that being over 50 is a drawback, it's bollocks. Enjoy it and ignore them.

Action 5: Start now

You might be thinking that this talk of opportunity for mature people is all well and good, but what do you do and where do you begin? If you really feel stuck in a rut, but terrified at the thought of starting something new or leaving, it might be because you're not quite sure what you'd rather be doing.

Ask yourself, 'What's important to me? What are my values? What do I enjoy doing and how can I turn that into a career? Brainstorm down all the new job options you have in terms of a change. Make sure the change will align to your values and what is important to you, and then take a reality check. As you look at each option, avoid the easy pessimistic road that will make you cross out all the alternatives. Yes be realistic, but not totally limiting.

As you look at the options, which ones excite you most? If they don't inspire or excite you, cross them off. Once you have done this, then rank each remaining option out of ten. Take the highest few and then rank again. If you are listening to your pathetic voice saying, 'Oh, I don't know', then get rid of that tone and just decide. Choose!

So, the choice is made. The choice fits your values, it excites you, it stimulates your brain and maybe other things, so it is time to write down all the proactive things you need to do to make it happen. Some of these may be weekly and some may be monthly. For example, weekly may be to attend a college or university course. Monthly could be writing application letters explaining your interest to three prospective employers. Get the activtities listed and stick to them. These are your tactical actions, so make them happen.

Finally, what is the immediate task? Not next week, not tomorrow, but today. Perhaps it is to make a phone call to the local university for a prospectus and application form to enrol for a professional qualification, or to fill in an application to become a member of a professional organisation so you receive their monthly journals. Or perhaps it is simply to call a specialist recruitment agency and make an appointment to meet them. There's plenty you can do to take the first step, and all you 'silver surfers' can take the lead by going online and looking at job search sites, careers advice and info sites for professional bodies etc. Come on, get on and do it, because action brings the result.

Real Life

Irene

Irene was a 45-year-old senior administrator, and after 20 years in the job she was totally bored and wanted much more from life and work.

Her values included support, respect and ambition for others and she identified that teaching was the career she wanted to move into. To do this, she saved for two years, and at the age of 47 went to study full-time for a PGCE.

Irene used her maturity and experience to be really good at classroom management. She was already confident compared to other junior teachers, whose average age was 22 and who were very wet behind the ears. Within two months of leaving her course, she was appointed to a teaching post in an all-girls school.

She's now head of department and, at the age of 54, she is determined to go to the top and become head of the school.

Martin

As a 53-year-old sales manager, Martin had put in over 20 years with the same employer. He knew he wanted a change, but didn't know how to get out and do something else.

He identified his priorities and values as: support for people, fairness, and integrity. Martin made it clear that money was not what motivated him any more, but what he really wanted was a job with a charity that changed other people's lives for the better.

He decided that he wanted to become a fundraising manager. To achieve this goal he enrolled on an HND course in public sector management and networked with colleagues on the course to build up his knowledge and contacts.

He noted down all his skills and experience and how these would support a charity and its work. It took a little time, but, being experienced, he didn't mind the wait. A year after his course, Martin identified the charity he wanted to work for and when a suitable post came up he was offered an interview. He was successfully appointed as fundraising manager for a national charity working on overseas aid and development projects.

There's no doubt in my mind that we have come into an 'age of experience' where the experience and knowledge of older generations is not only to be valued, but is vital. When it comes to the job market, I think we are already seeing businesses take stock of the talent that's available and they are recruiting older candidates.

I'm quite envious of you, if you're over 50, because you have so much in front of you and you've come through the majority of life's challenges. You've done the career/careers, maybe raised a family, bought the house etc., and now you can choose more freely what it is you want to do.

All I ask is that you keep your mind open and do not think for a minute that no one wants what you have to offer because you are mature. It's not acceptable for you to think this, nor for anyone who's out there. We need you more than ever!

Job Grabber check list

- ○ Are you content to be retired?
- ○ Follow the Get Off Your Arse action plan for mature applicants
- ○ Align the job you go for with your values
- ○ List all your experience
- ○ Don't take no for an answer

Women come back to work

The challenge

Women returning to work, having taken years out to bring up the kids, can have a bit of a tough time convincing employers they have not only the skills and knowledge to do the job but also the commitment. Employers will have concerns that little Johnny or Lizzy are going to be, quite rightly, your priority when you come back to work, and being off because they are sick every few weeks is not going to go down well. As an entrepreneur myself, I have some sympathy for this concern, although one needs to realise that it is the minority of women returners who knowingly take the piss.

When my colleague and friend Joanna Simmons had her child at the age of 34 she had already built up a successful career as a solicitor. She decided to take a career break for three years while raising her newborn. Joanna didn't want to miss out on these important years. She left on good terms with her former employer, but, understandably, they could not commit to keeping her job open for that period of time.

When Joanna hit her 37th birthday, she made the conscious decision to go back to work. Arranging childcare would prove expensive, but she knew she had to return. I remember explaining to Joanna that she needed to realise having a baby was her responsibility and no one else's, so she couldn't expect employers to bend over backwards for her. She swallowed my candid opinion and, thankfully, we remained friends!

Joanna realised that finding new employment was not as easy as she had hoped. For several months she rarely received an invite to interview, and when she did she was unsuccessful. She had high expectations and wanted a well-paid solicitor's job that would once again challenge her brain and utilise her skills. What Joanna didn't want to do was work 60 hours a week again, because family life was now her immediate focus.

The barriers for Joanna were concrete and she had lost the knack of promoting herself well. She had to wake up and realise that if there were two applicants, one of whom was currently employed and the other had had a three-year gap, the employer would most likely take the former. The harsh reality was that her experience was three years out of date and she was going to be in a weaker position.

Furthermore, stating that she didn't want to work long hours was not helping her corner. Most employers like to see a real commitment and these comments were obviously detrimental to her application. Speaking your mind through your heart is not always the best approach at an interview. Engage your brain before you start talking about what you 'need' from the job.

Employers are often worried about divided priorities and will equate long hours with hard work. You have to be fair and see the employer's view – that they want to be sure the job will be done and done well. They expect a high degree of commitment to the job so that you deliver the goods for them. This is the case whether you are an experienced solicitor like Joanna, or a store manager who has to reach a host of performance and sales targets. Employers want your mind on the job.

So, in a time when we have legislation and the practical support that have shaped family-friendly policies I ask, 'Are they really working?' I guess for some companies the answer is 'Yes, very well' and for others 'Not really, and we don't like them'. So what's the answer, girls? How are we going to get you back into work? Don't worry, I'll explain.

1: Persistence, girls

It can, and probably will, take time to find a new role that equates to the one you left, especially if you want to return part-time or on a job-share basis. It's likely that you will receive a pile of rejection letters, and will have your confidence knocked more than once.

The modern labour market, however, requires employers to be more flexible when it comes to employing their human resources to meet their commercial goals, so that's on your side.

Never give up, girls; expect the knock-backs but keep going and fight for what you deserve.

2: Lazy bitch? Erm, no!!!

Take a really good look at what you have been doing while bringing up the kids. During your time out you will have developed new skills and behaviours often in demand from employers. The point here is transferability of your skills and experience. Looking after children, I imagine, will have developed those 'soft skills' – the patience, communication and interpersonal skills and time management skills – all of which are required by modern day executives. Perhaps you have been involved in organising activities with other mums, and negotiating with suppliers of baby products. Write all this down. Have you been a lazy bitch? I really doubt it very much.

3: Update your skills now

Having time out will probably mean your IT skills have become a bit rusty. Most jobs now use some form of modern technology, so I am afraid, girls, it is a case of cutting those nails and getting your fingers on the keyboard again. You may well have continued learning at home on your own computer, so that's good stuff. You must understand the internet, email, and common packages like Word, at the very least. If you already do, then get learning something new such as PowerPoint and Excel. Furthermore, if you have any additional skills to update, get on and do it.

4: Get support in order

Returning to work will mean you need to give consideration to your work–life balance. You are going to have to manage the new job, and the demands it will bring, as well as the kids and the other half. Sit down and talk to the other half, and if they aren't willing to support you, then you have three choices.

The first is that you don't bother going back to work and you let your mind become jelly. The second is that you enlist support from relatives or friends to look after the kids – or you could of course pay for childcare if you can afford it. And the final option is to separate or get divorced. If the partner is holding you back and you can't work it out, my advice is to fuck 'em off!

5: CV gap covered

Update your CV, following my guidelines described in Chapter 15. When you come to the gap covering your career break, fill it in with the soft-skill competencies developed during that time. This will help camouflage the length of time you were out of the job market, and will demonstrate that you have continued developing, albeit out of the corporate world. It also shows that you have initiative and intelligence. It's not just a disguise: it's a way to present the real life skills you have called on to bring up the kids.

6: Glam up, girls!

Now, a lot of you ladies do let yourselves go a bit when you have the little ones, so step up and let's get you into shape. If you have piled on the fat, get it off! It is ugly and I will have none of your beauty hidden by the flab trap. Go and buy *Get Off Your Arse and Lose Weight*. It will sort you out in no time. Treat yourself to a consultation with a stylist and act on his or her recommendations. Look in that wardrobe and chuck out the mumsy rubbish that makes you look as if you go to Minorca half board every year. That's right – let's get glam!

7: Become the interviewer's dream

Now, get practising your interview techniques. Have a look at some of the questions and answers outlined in Chapter 17 to help you model your own answers. Do practise explaining to the interviewer how having a career break has developed additional skill sets. And never, ever say that you are looking for a work–life balance and that your priorities have changed. It won't help you, darling! Let the interviewer know how you are committed to re-establishing your career, and that your focus is on attaining a job that will stretch your brain and also add value to the business and the bottom line.

8: Don't piss everyone off

Now, I would like to offer a word of warning for when you get the new job. Avoid talking about the kids too much. It really does get on many people's nerves and they will talk about you behind your back. Yes, people in the main love children, but equally there is a huge proportion who have no interest whatsoever in what the little one had for his breakfast or did at school. And, of course, do your best to avoid being late and leaving early because of the kids. It will piss a lot of people off, although they won't say it to your face. The key is to get organised before you even apply for a job.

Real Life

Annabel

Returning to the workplace at the age of 32 after a five-year career break, Annabel wanted to get back into the world where she had been a senior graphic designer.

She had two major challenges to overcome; one was that in her time out she'd not really picked up her mouse and switched on the Mac, but had concentrated her time on the kids. This meant she wasn't up with the latest packages and technology. The second problem was the fact that she had become a lone parent, and didn't have the family back-up or resources to get childcare in place.

With these significant blocks, Annabel wasn't sure that she'd stand any chance of getting back into the job she was really passionate about. I'd been talking to her and put her in touch with a contact of mine who runs a graphic design business. He offered to give Annabel the chance to come in for a couple of days per week and act as an assistant on a nominal salary. It allowed her to brush up her graphic design skills while working around school drop-off and pick-up times.

Bolstered by this experience, and with a few other pointers, Annabel was able to get financial support to buy her own computer and software equipment and to set up as a freelance graphic designer from her home. She's her own boss, working on projects for my contact and others, earning her own living and raising the kids. Everybody is happy.

Stacey

At 56 Stacey had brought up her son and packed him off to university. The only problem was that she'd not had a job for over 18 years, and had no idea of what she could do in the world of work.

At the same time as being excited at the prospect of going out to work Stacey was scared to death of failing to get a job and then of not actually being good enough to hold onto it.

She came to see me after being referred by a mutual friend, who thought that she needed a one-to-one to work on her image and motivation. Well, we started by auditing what her qualifications and experience had been and identifying what it was that she really wanted to do.

She realised that she really wanted to work with older, vulnerable people, partly because she'd got a degree in sociology, but also because she'd cared for her own parents and thought that there was a lack of motivated people looking after our elderly. The solution we agreed was that she should train to become a social worker, specialising in working with the elderly.

She went away and identified organisations that could offer her a job and potential sponsorship to go through the academic study that would give her the social work qualification she needed.

With Stacey, I also helped her to sharpen her image and personal presentation, so that she would bowl over any interview panel. I'm happy to report that she was taken on by a local authority and is now a social work team supervisor, working with older people.

So there you have it, girls, the world *will* open up to you as a woman returning to work after raising children. The door might feel a bit stuck at times, but if you plan, are persistent and resilient, and are prepared to give it a boot, there is every chance that you will get back into the world of work at the level you want. Remember, the hardest thing to do is overcome the preconceptions of the recruiter, especially if they are a bit old-school. That said, I do appreciate their concerns. Employers do have a business to run so be sympathetic to that.

Job Grabber *check list*

- Get over the knock-backs asap
- Bring your skills and qualifications as up to date as possible
- Be prepared to deal with preconceptions and stereotypical attitudes
- Accept that employers have reasonable expectations about you

Getting on top 14

What a lovely place to be – right at the very top of the tree. You can look down and see what a great job you and everyone else is doing. How marvellous, my darlings!

Reaching the top of your career ladder or profession can be rewarding on a variety of levels; you have extra kudos, pride in your position, power and control to make decisions, satisfaction in knowing you are steering the particular ship that you are on, and of course, potentially, a much higher salary and bigger rewards package.

However, not everyone wants to get to the top. So, if you're one of those, you might want to read this and find out what makes those at the top tick, or else you could sod off and move on to the next chapter.

For many, the thought of being promoted to a senior role is the ultimate goal of being in a job. In this chapter, I will guide you through a number of processes to help get you there. And as the world changes, boy, it's nice to see more women shoving men out of the way to get there. For example, consider my colleague and personal friend Penny, who came from an ordinary background like me to become eventually the managing director of a restaurant chain.

Not only did she work hard and carry out daily actions in support of her career ambitions, but she managed the male egos so well. We know times are changing, and men are at last realising that to pigeonhole women in stereotypical ways is not only wrong but also very yesterday. I have always thought that men who display such ridiculous attitudes must have small endowments, so they make up for it with having a big gob which they engage before the brain.

My rant's nearly over, but, hey girls, now is the time to let these so-called boys know that you are equally capable, and often in my opinion, more competent, and certainly more emotionally intelligent. This last, in my view, is more useful for business success than general IQ. Of course, guys, most of you are the modern-day man, so don't get the hump if women are competing with, and beating, you.

Senior males in business these days are grasping the concept of equality and emotional intelligence. Either that or more men are growing in the tackle department!

Right, let's get on with getting you to the top of the career tower or your job ladder.

Process 1: Work hard from day one

Obvious yes, but I am not simply referring to the practical outputs of your job. Be sure to carry a positive attitude and conduct yourself professionally in the discharge of all your duties. Keep your eyes on the goal, and never take your foot off the gas. Employers want to promote people and give opportunities and responsibilities to those who apply themselves, have a spark and who are proactive.

You want to be labelled as someone who works hard and gets a job done to everyone's satisfaction. Monitor your own attitude, and ensure you look the business as well as talk the business in what you do. Yes, be smart – and that means in the head as well as in appearance and contribution. Remember the Henry Ford quote at all times: 'The harder I work, the luckier I become.'

We have all heard the 'urban legends' of Ted who started in the post room and who's now chairman of a multi-national, or Gladys whose first role with the company was as a PA and who now has a 30 per cent stake in the business. There are people who literally do rise from the shop floor and go on to take control of a company, and they are brilliant examples of what hard work can achieve.

Process 2: Play the game

It's a fact that to win the game you have to be a player in it. This means that you show support for company-wide decisions at all times and you keep your mouth well and truly closed if you find the MD on top of the office desk with their PA! We often see and hear things in our jobs that turn our stomachs or make us angry because we don't agree with them, but there's a time and a place to make yourself heard – and, unless you're near or at the top, it's not now.

Here's how to play the game:

- In meetings be sure to contribute, and make all contributions in the interests of moving the business forward. Get to know as many people at the top as you can and, yes, make yourself smile, say good morning and get into conversation with them.

- Be one of those who stays late, and always attend company functions. Oh, and at company functions forget having a grope with any of your colleagues or staff. People do talk.
- Go out of your way to help others out, especially if they are one of the 'in' gang with the directors. It will soon come to pass that your reputation, in other words your personal branding, is of someone who is helpful, professional, hardworking and, of course, very company minded.

As one final thought, do draw the line at sleeping your way to the top. It is seedy and vile and, believe me, one day it will backfire and you will get found out. You don't want to have your face splashed all over the *News of the World*, do you?

Process 3: Be charismatic

Developing your personal presence, or charisma, is important in helping you get to the top. You need to stand out from the crowd in a way that makes you attractive to be around. You don't need to put on a clown suit and big shoes, or suddenly start talking in what you think is an authoritative voice. No, my dears, there are more subtle ways to show charisma.

When you have got charisma, people will want to be around you. You will become a magnet and will attract the company movers and shakers who will be instrumental in your steady climb up the corporate ladder, unless of course you are totally shit at your job.

I am going to give you four top tips to develop your charisma:

- From this moment, walk tall and smile with those eyes. Dress like a real catch, but not totally tarty please.
- Empathise and engage with everyone. Yes, everyone! Charismatic people talk to everyone from the so-called 'menial' at the bottom to the chief executive at the top. Status isn't an issue for truly charismatic people.
- Think charisma and show your passion. Keep thinking in your mind that you are charismatic and allow those thoughts to be with you constantly.
- Show your passion for the company and its people – but never take your passion for the boardroom through to the bedroom with one of your bosses.

Just to recap then, understand what being a charismatic person means and that having this outwardly displayed as part of your character will help you to rise naturally to the top. Go on, put a big smile on your face and walk tall.

Process 4: Initiate business advancement

Have your own think tank session at least once a month. List as many ideas as possible of how the organisation can be in better shape, increase productivity, drive customer service and sales revenues, or be an employer of choice.

Evaluate the ideas and select one that should at some point be presented to senior decision makers. Think it through before you present it. Have your arguments for initiation and be sure that you can explain the commercial gain to the organisation. Any idea should be able to contribute to cost savings or increasing revenues, either directly or indirectly.

Think through how to present your ideas. Presenting face-to-face has to be your first choice, because you can explain the idea in full at the same time as displaying your charisma. Your audience will also have the opportunity to clarify any points of concern. Do this a few times a year and before long you will become one of the senior gang.

Process 5: Be the inspirational leader

Who is going to promote a leader who is unable to inspire the hungry to break bread? This is why you have to concentrate on building yourself into an inspirational leader. Here's how you can do it:

- Set and share your business goals and vision with your team. Deliver these at a team presentation every six months.
- Once the vision is shared, sit down with each of your direct reports and set them objectives. Their objectives will support the vision you have shared with the full team.
- Each month hold one-to-one personal meetings with your team and monitor performance.
- Coach both your team as a whole and individual members of the team to develop their skills and behaviours.
- Be proactive with poor performance. If coaching doesn't work and you have offered all reasonable support possible, then discipline is the answer. And, yes, don't be afraid to dismiss someone. Sometimes it is the only answer.

- Celebrate achievement with the team and offer incentives. Consider having an employee of the month, team awards, or if one of your team has done something exceptional, then draft a letter of thanks for what has been achieved and get the MD to sign it.

Process 6: Never stop learning

Learning is a lifetime project, so don't get up your arse thinking no one can teach you anything new. Believe me, they can! As you climb the corporate ladder ensure you develop your strategic thinking. Consider a Diploma in Management Studies, or an MBA, or attend programmes offered by the Institute of Directors. Alternatively, if there is no budget, then get some books and do some reading around management, leadership and the skills you need at the top such as the financials of running a business. Developing yourself isn't just about getting your arse in a classroom, it's about learning from those around you and looking further afield to develop your talents.

One of the best ways to develop yourself is to source a role model. Select someone who displays inspirational behaviours and has the experience you require. Learn from them and if possible meet with them once a month. You may have to pay for the lunches yourself but, believe me, it is worth every penny. Make sure you get their guidance and insights into reaching the top, there's no such thing as a free lunch! I'm not talking about nipping down to McDonald's. Don't be a cheapskate, you are out to impress and glean information so go to a decent restaurant.

Real Life

Nasreen

Nasreen is a 30-year-old IT manager with ambitions to reach the top working in a medium sized business employing around 500 staff.

She joined the company after leaving university and went on to gain an MBA from one of the UK's top business schools, using her own time and resources. She knew the MBA would give her the broader understanding of the different elements to building, running and expanding a successful business.

When she hit 28 she became very ambitious and set her goal to become the IT Director as there wasn't one on the board and she knew she could do it. She'd got the MBA and had the experience within the company to drive things forward.

Nasreen realised she had to develop sound relationships with the directors above her and made it her goal to offer a business idea every two months to the MD via email and present them to her boss who was the Operations Director.

She selected me to become her role model and met with me once a month. Working together, we developed her charisma and leadership capability to inspire and create business benefits. Taking on the actions of Process 3 and 5 outlined above, Nasreen developed not only her personal presence but also her ability to lead the IT team.

She went out of her way to learn to play golf as she was aware the directors enjoyed this as a business and leisure opportunity. Slightly up the arse I know, but it worked. She got to know the MD much better and within six months of us working together made it clear to her boss she was hungry for directorship. Nasreen was awarded the new role soon after and is now playing the game to be next in line for MD.

Bridget

Bridget, a 41-year-old Customer Service Manager, was working at a large telecommunications company. All the directors were male and she described the culture as macho, but full of men with real insecurities.

In the past, Bridget acknowledged, she had been a little too open with her own line manager who was the Customer Service Director. She had made her feelings known about the culture, which at the time she described as testosterone fuelled mania! She soon realised this would get her nowhere, and she wanted to plan a strategy to grab a directorship as her boss was nearing retirement.

Bridget enrolled, with the support of the company, on a series of courses through the Institute of Directors which she knew would develop her strategic thinking and business etiquette.

During this time she kept her head down and worked incredibly hard and her dedication helped to reduce customer complaints by 20 per cent. She ensured she communicated her ideas on how to build a more customer-focused business with the MD. She was invited to present her ideas to the board. All the while, she remained her assertive self but knew she also had to become one of the boys. She would need to laugh at their humour and later vomit in the toilet.

What Bridget had done so well was to play the game. She loved the business and was a genuinely inspiring leader. As retirement came for her boss, she applied for the role and confidently requested that the MD give her six months to prove herself in the role. Not only did she get the opportunity, but after only three months she was appointed permanently to the position.

Getting to the top can involve climbing a slippery pole, and you may receive one or two knock-backs on the way, but I have shown you that getting to the top can be done with some determination, planning and game playing. There are shortcuts to getting to the top, but buying your way, or sleeping your way, to the top can bring some nasty surprises.

You should also carefully consider if being at the top of an organisation is actually what you want to do. It's just an accepted aspiration for many people who plod up a career ladder, but then find themselves in a position where they don't want to be because of the added pressures and responsibilities. Think hard before you make a decision to go to the top.

What I want you to do is to decide if getting to the top will float your boat. What do you anticipate getting from this journey? In my view, it's the sense of achieving something that others haven't. That's what drives me. If it drives you too, go on, get your arse to the top.

Job Grabber check list

- Are you cut out to get to the top?
- Be prepared for a lifetime of learning
- Play the game

You selling you – the CV 15

There are many tricks and tips to putting together a 'perfect CV', but I'm going to give you my take on this document which can sell you and open doors.

You should see your Curriculum Vitae or 'CV' as an advert to sell yourself to a potential employer. The purpose of your CV is to showcase you, your relevant skills and experience, attributes and background in a brief written form. It has to present you as capable, interesting and worth considering by the company or organisation you are contacting with the aim of landing a job interview or invitation to an assessment centre.

Selling yourself really well before the face-to-face meeting is critical, as it will give you an edge over other applicants provided you get it spot on. A prospective employer will often make a snap judgement the second they read your CV, and even highly qualified people can find themselves rejected if the CV fails to come up to scratch.

You must include the most relevant information which matches the job and person specifications for the post you want to get. Don't be a lazy slob and send the same CV out to everyone; it needs tailoring for each application to make sure you have bang-on what they are looking for. The other golden rule is: Don't make anything up. You'll eventually get caught and could get fired or worse.

CV wise words

The following points and examples are some straightforward advice to make sure you draft your CV correctly from the start. You need to get the basics spot-on before you start to design your CV, otherwise it will be a complete waste of time. Start by taking onboard the following:

- Make sure you use a good white/off-white paper to print your CV onto – no one wants to read from gaudy coloured paper, so don't get any fancy ideas.
- Do not attach extra documents such as qualifications as it looks messy. If the employer wants evidence of your qualifications, you will be asked to take them to the interview or post them if you are offered a job.
- Even if you think you look like Brad Pitt or Angelina Jolie, forget attaching stomach-turning photos of yourself, unless you're applying to be a glamour model or join MI6.
- Once you have designed the CV, check it several times. Perhaps ask a colleague or a friend to read it as well.
- Ensure there are no spelling mistakes or marks on it, as this will mean your CV is likely to end up in the bin.

- Follow the instructions from the job advert. If the employer requests four copies of your CV, then you should send four. Meet the deadline.
- The covering letter should also be customised for each job you apply for, as this is an additional opportunity to present a version of your skills tailored to what the employer requires.
- The CV should be no longer than two sides of A4.

So what should be included on a really good CV? I recommend six sections, but remember to tailor each CV and covering letter to what the job requires. The sections outlined here are in the recommendsd sequential order.

Personal details

Include your full name, address, contact telephone numbers, driving licence details, and email address. Never put down your age, marital status and details of children. It is unlawful for employers to discriminate on these areas, but there are still some short-sighted, ignorant recruiters out there who discriminate on these grounds, so, to be sure, keep them off.

Personal objective

Here you can highlight your career objective by providing a couple of sentences that explain your aspirations and ambitions. Of course, these must be relevant to the job for which you are applying. The objective may cover the next job move but also the kind of environment you want to move to.

Take a look at these examples:

Steve Miller

'To attain a position working in a charity organisation supporting the delivery of help to people with special needs'

'To attain a senior sales role with people management responsibility within the chemicals sector'

'To achieve a senior management role responsible for the strategic development of product lines and customer service'

Education and qualifications

It is useful to bullet point your education and qualifications in chronological order. It may be appropriate to list just higher education and professional qualifications. This will depend upon your age and experience. For example, someone in their 20s may be well advised to put down all their qualifications whilst someone who is in their 40s may well just put down the latter years of education.

Experience

Employers will be particularly interested in this area. List your experience over the last ten years and include your achievements in each role. Make sure you skew your experience to match what the advertisement states the job requires. Take a look at the CV samples on the pages that follow to help you lay out your experience.

Special achievements and interests

It is really advisable to put down details of any achievements that are related to your application. For example, if you won sales person of the year then put it down. Or you may have been selected by your employer to head a project as a result of your special abilities. When it comes to interests I would say keep them brief and simple. Avoid a long list that may bore the recruiter.

References

Include two references, but please not the local vicar! References should be your current line manager or director. However, if you are a college or university graduate ask the academic staff to provide a professional reference.

Sample CV 1 – Application for the position of Telesales Executive for a mobile phone company

PERSONAL DETAILS

Name: Samantha Smith

Address: 30 Chester Street, Derby, DR2 0TH

Telephone: 01332 0000000 or 00000 000000 (m)

Email: samanthasmith@lifebitchmail.com

Driving Licence: Full, Clean

PERSONAL OBJECTIVE

To successfully attain a sales position, having recently graduated from Manchester University, and ideally working within a fast paced retail environment.

EDUCATION AND QUALIFICATIONS

- 1999–2004: Derbyshire School for Girls: GCSE passes in Mathematics (B); English Language (A); Physics (C); History (A); Art (C); Social Science (B); Drama (B)
- 2004–2006: Derbyshire College of Further Education: A Level passes in English (B); Drama (A); Sociology (B)
- 2006–2009: Manchester University: BA (Hons) English and Drama Upper Second Class Degree

Steve Miller

EXPERIENCE

Employer	Dates	Job Title
	Achievements	
Manchester Student Union	2006 to 2009	Bar Person
	– Successfully managed customer complaints	

SPECIAL ACHIEVEMENTS AND INTERESTS

In 2004 I achieved my Duke of Edinburgh Gold award. My interests include holding dinner parties with friends and I have a particular interest in popular psychology. I have travelled extensively and especially enjoy eastern culture.

REFERENCES

Mr J Dawson	Professor M Mitchell
Bar and Restaurant Manager	Department of English and Drama
Manchester University	Manchester University
1 Manchester Road	1 Manchester Road
Manchester	Manchester
M1 1AT	M1 1AT

Sample CV 2 – Application for the Position of Accounts Manager

---

PERSONAL DETAILS

Name: Justin Chalmers

Address: 12 Kingsbury Road, Southampton, SR2 1GG

Telephone: 023 000000 or 00000 000000 (m)

Email: chalmers123@lifebitchmail.com

Driving Licence: Full, Clean

PERSONAL OBJECTIVE

To lead, coach and develop a team of accounts and credit control assistants within a blue chip motoring organisation with an emphasis on ABC1 customers.

EDUCATION AND QUALIFICATIONS

- 1994–1998: Southampton Shires Comprehensive: GCSE passes in Mathematics (A); English Language (C); Statistics (A); History (D); Technical Drawing (C); Drama (D)
- 1998–2000: Derbyshire College of Further Education: A Levels passes in Accounting (B); Statistics (D); Mathematics (C)
- 2000–2003: Huddersfield University: BA (Hons) Business and Finance Lower Second

EXPERIENCE (LAST 5 YEARS)

Employer	Dates Achievements	Job Title
Andrews PLC	2003–2005	Accounts Assistant
	– Produced monthly invoices accurately	
	– Maintained customer accounts successfully	

Steve Miller

– Increased sales by using initiative

– Acted as Team Captain as requested by line manager

– Organised drinks promotions to support average customer spend

– Counted petty cash and generated reports for head office

Andrews PLC	2005 – Date	Senior Accountant

– Managed year end and prepared accounts with FD

– Recruited the team of accounts assistants

– Performance managed a team of 3 accounts assistants

– Led and coached the performance of the accounts team

– Provided accurate and timely financial management information

– Updated and provided full year forecasts

– Managed and coached the credit controller

SPECIAL ACHIEVEMENTS AND INTERESTS

Interests include 5-a-side football, racket sports and organising charity events for the British Heart Foundation.

REFERENCES

Mr J Taylor	Mrs H Edwards
Financial Director	Director
Andrews PLC	British Heart Foundation
1 Hugh Road	2 Crest Road
Southampton	Southampton
S12 9BG	S32 9HY

Sample CV 3 – Application for the position of Charity Co-ordinator

---

PERSONAL DETAILS

Name: Angela Mason

Address: 3 The Place, Glasgow, GL3 9YY

Telephone: 0141 0000000 or 00000 000000 (m)

Email: matt222@lifebitchmail.com

Driving Licence: Full, Clean

PERSONAL OBJECTIVE

To return to work having had two children and attain a full time administrative position working within the public sector, ideally within a charity organisation

EDUCATION AND QUALIFICATIONS

- 2000–2002: Glasgow College of Further Education: B/TEC National Certificate in Business and Finance
- 2007–Date: BA degree in Public Sector Management

EXPERIENCE (LAST 10 YEARS)

Employer	Dates Achievements	Job Title
Glasgow Sheltered Housing	1999–2004	Office Manager
	Key Achievements:	
	– Assisted in processing social housing applications	
	– Managed customer complaints and the appeals process	
	– Produced monthly application reports for the management team	

– Successfully set up a new database for customer records

– Reduced the overheads by 15% by introducing preferred supplier tenders

– Increased the profile of the organisation by taking on PR responsibilities

– Co-ordinated the charity events administered by the organisation

SPECIAL ACHIEVEMENTS AND INTERESTS

Achieved student of the year status upon completion of B/TEC National Certificate in Business and Finance

REFERENCES

Mary Stone	Mr S Simpson
General Manager	Head of Business Studies
Glasgow Sheltered Housing	Glasgow College of Further Education
1 North Street	Kings Town Road
Glasgow	Glasgow
G11 8TT	G4 7YT

Sample CV 4 – Application for the position of Senior PR Executive

PERSONAL DETAILS

Name: Emma Shannon

Address: 24 Avenue Road, Birmingham, B16 7UY

Telephone: 0121 000 0000 or 00000 000000 (m)

Email: Emma101@lifebitchmail.com

Driving Licence: Full, Clean

PERSONAL OBJECTIVE

To attain a PR Executive role within a London based agency specialising in entertainment and celebrity management

EDUCATION AND QUALIFICATIONS

- 2001–2004: University of Bedfordshire: B.A (Hons) Upper Second Degree in Marketing
- 2005–2006 CIPR Postgraduate Diploma in Public Relations

EXPERIENCE (LAST 10 YEARS)

Employer	Dates Achievements	Job Title
PR Revolution	2006–Date	PR Account Manager
	– Managed a client base of 20 within the B2B sector	
	– Successfully won 9 new accounts in last 12 months	
	– Prepared all client press releases	
	– Successfully retained and renewed all client contracts year on year	

– Successfully achieved national and international PR hits for clients in a wide range of broadcast, print, online media

– Developed and nurtured editorial contacts for business publications

– Successfully arranged celebrity endorsement for 6 clients

PR Revolution	2004–2006	PR Executive

– Assisted the PR Account managers in developing editorial opportunities for clients

– Prepared press releases and case study features with Account Managers

– Contributed to the business pitch with Key Account Managers

– Prepared monthly client activity reports

– Managed the administration for client celebrity endorsement

SPECIAL ACHIEVEMENTS AND INTERESTS

I achieved Distinction status in my final CIPR examinations. I am currently involved in producing a screenplay and enjoy racket sports.

REFERENCES

Mr I Pole	Mrs G Appleby
Managing Director	Head of Business School
PR Revolution	Bedfordshire University
12 Lee Street	12 Bedford Road
Birmingham	Bedford
B91 6TY	B11 88Y

Covering letters

Do not send in a CV without a well-thought-out covering letter either in a hard copy or electronic format. Please bear in mind that companies and organisations that just get your CV will assume, quite correctly, that you are bone idle. If you don't send a covering letter that's tailored to the job you are applying for, it shows them, and me, that you haven't got any extra drive and intelligence. The same goes for sending out a speculative CV to hundreds of potential employers. Each has to have a tailored covering letter that shows you know something about them, and explains why you would make a great fit into their organisation.

Covering letters should be kept brief and punchy to really grab the attention of the person who reads it. Whenever possible, try to find the name of the person who will be dealing with applications and CVs, and address your letter, plus the envelope, to that person by name.

The letter is the tool that will draw the recruiter/potential employer into reading your CV, so make it relevant, interesting and very well presented: definitely no mistakes, smudges or tatty paper. It has got to appear slick and clean.

If you are sending in a speculative CV, hoping that they may have work for you, explain what sort of work you are interested in. Then go on to outline your key skills and experience that align you to that type of role and show how you'd fit into their set-up. If you send a speculative CV, always telephone later to push your enquiry further and make sure your information gets into the right hands.

When drafting the content of your covering letter, it is useful to draw the recruiter's attention to particular parts of your CV such as pertinent experience or outstanding achievements.

Start your letter with an underlined heading giving the job title you are interested in and where you sourced the job lead or company/organisation information from.

Take a look at the four examples below that would support each of the CVs set out on the previous pages.

SAMPLE LETTER 1

Dear Mrs Osborne,

RE: Application for the Position of Telesales Executive

I am pleased to enclose my CV for the position of Telesales Executive as advertised in the Derby Chronicle. As you will see from my CV I have recently graduated from Manchester University having completed a degree in English and Drama. In addition to a sound academic background I also offer several years of sales and customer experience with specific capabilities including:

1. Up-selling and cross-selling
2. Meeting the needs of customers
3. Selling specific promotions to achieve business targets

With a sound background in a sales and customer service environment I would be keen to meet in person to discuss my application in more detail.

Yours sincerely,

Samantha Smith

SAMPLE LETTER 2

Dear Mr James,

RE: Application for the Position of Accounts Manager

Further to your recent advertisement posted on totaljobs.com please find attached my CV. The CV highlights my professional achievements to date which include:

1. Management experience for a team of three accounts assistants who also carried out credit control responsibilities
2. Recruitment and performance management experience
3. Experience of managing year end accounts as requested in your advertisement
4. Financial forecasting and head office reporting
5. Full ACCA Membership

With solid professional experience I am keen to join an organisation offering the opportunity to manage the accounts function including credit control. Based on my background I am confident I bring the required competencies to perform the role. I would welcome the opportunity to meet with you to review my capabilities and achievements.

Yours sincerely,

Justin Chalmers

SAMPLE LETTER 3

Dear Mrs Parker,

RE: Application for the position of Charity Co-ordinator

Having read with interest your advertisement in Charity Times for the position of Charity Co-ordinator I am delighted to enclose my CV for your consideration.

I recently completed a career break and I am now very keen to return to the world of work and attain a role that will utilise my professional experience. I feel the role of Charity Co-ordinator aligns itself closely to both my aspirations and previous experience. In particular I am pleased to offer:

1. Previous experience managing a number of projects for a charity organisation
2. Experience in providing a full administration service to the charity
3. Comprehensive experience co-ordinating fund raising events and volunteer applications

In addition to my previous experience I am also pleased to draw your attention to my recent academic achievement passing a BTEC National Diploma in Business and Finance and receiving the special award of Student of the Year for outstanding contribution and results.

I would now be keen to move to the next stage of the application process and would welcome the opportunity to meet with you in order to outline the specific aligned experience that I will bring to the role in addition to my passion to support a local charity.

Yours sincerely,

Angela Mason

SAMPLE LETTER 4

Dear Mr Hill,

<u>RE: Application for the Position of Senior PR Executive</u>

I am pleased to enclose my CV for the position of Senior PR Executive. As you will note from my experience I have an impressive background working within an energetic PR environment. In addition to notable academic achievements I bring experience aligned to your needs including:

1 Experience of building and managing a large client portfolio

2 Managing celebrity PR for business clients

3 Developing strong editorial contacts

Given my background and its match to your requirements I look forward to meeting with you to discuss my application in greater depth.

Yours sincerely,

Emma Shannon

To help you know where to look to find the job that you want to grab see the appendix at the end of the book, which lists print and online job sources.

Job Grabber *check list*

- Look at the CV and covering letter samples
- Keep to relevant facts and tailor your CV for each job
- Have you included the six recommended CV sections?
- Write an individual covering letter for each application
- Make sure that each final CV is well presented, clean and spell-checked

Preparation is everything – the interview

16

nterview preparation is absolutely critical. If you can't be arsed to prepare, then don't even bother going to the interview because either your heart isn't in it, or you're simply lazy. It might seem as if it's a waste of time, or you're so fucking clever that you never need to prepare for anything, but, believe me, that's utter crap. I know many bright and intelligent people who think they can 'wing it' when it comes to interviews and they usually end falling on their arse.

Preparation includes many areas such as your appearance, state of mind/attitude, and of course your knowledge about the job and the organisation that could be your new employer. Probably the best way to find out more than the basics given in a job specification or advert is to ask for company brochures and information before you are interviewed or find out more from the internet.

The really great thing about preparing well is that it will make you feel more self-assured and confident. You will know you understand what the job you are being interviewed for requires, have a great knowledge of the company, and be ready for questions. You'll feel better, perform better and be inspirational to those who you meet during the interviews.

Now let's take a look at the areas you will need to prepare so that you are in the best possible shape for an interview.

Prep 1 – The employer

Employers will want to feel that you have made an effort to find out about them. And you can't blame them! Who wants some nerd on board who couldn't be fagged to find out a few facts? Just picture the episodes of *The Apprentice* where the final candidates get down to one-on-one interviews with Sir Alan Sugar's advisers and there are always a few who couldn't be arsed to bone up on his companies. Needless to say, they don't get offered the job.

The more information you have, the easier it will be for you to tailor your interview responses to show the interviewer that you are the ideal person for the job. It's always impressed me when I've interviewed people who know about my own organisation, the clients we have, and what our culture is. It shows they understand the company and want to be a part of it.

As a guide I would suggest you find out about the following:

- What sort of organisation are they? What are their current services or products?
- What are the company's vision, mission and values?

- What future plans do they have?
- Approximately how many staff does the organisation employ?
- Who are their competitors? What advantages does this organisation have over their competitors?
- From this research can you bring any ideas to the table that would add to the competitive advantage of your prospective employer?
- Who are the organisation's customers?
- What locations do they have? Are they a one-site or multi-site organisation?
- Who is the Chief Executive or Managing Director?
- If they are a stock exchange listed company, how is their share price performing?

Prep 2 – Selling you

The interview is often a relaxed meeting, quite informal and friendly, but do remember that the interviewer is selecting the best person for the job, so don't be fooled into thinking halfway through the meeting that you are getting on so well it gives you the opportunity to ask the interviewer out on a date or to go and have a cigarette together! It is about how you sell yourself so that you professionally demonstrate you have the skills, knowledge, attitudes and behaviours to perform the job competently.

In effect the interview is a sales pitch. And, as I well know, before you can do a sales pitch, you need to understand and believe in your product. Solid preparation must be conducted so that you understand the value of you in relation to the job. The product in this case is

Steve Miller

YOU! Get yourself a notebook right now and record your answers to the following questions:

- What skills do you have specifically that are required for the job?
- What three key achievements do you have that are directly related to the job?
- What areas of further development would you have if you were to be offered the job?
- How does your personality style fit into the job and you being good at it?
- Why should this employer recruit you for this role?
- What practical examples do you have that demonstrate you have the experience to do this job well?
- What are you most proud of in your career to date?
- Why should an employer want you to work for them?

Prep 3 – Boost the belief

As soon as you apply for a job that you have your heart set on, ensure that you carry out one or two of the techniques outlined in Chapter 6. Your belief structure needs to be rock solid so just make sure you get on and do them. People griping about nerves before interviews do so because they have simply been too lazy to do anything to boost their belief system.

Once you have increased your self-belief, the stronger you will be as you drive to the interview itself, meet the interviewer and perform well as they go through the interview process with you. I can't emphasise enough that getting your mind into shape with the techniques in Chapter 6 is vital to getting your character and confidence spot-on to get the job that you want and deserve. Don't skip past this and think it's a load of mumbo jumbo. If you do, you will not be in shape to get through any interview, tough or not, because you will not know how it will pan out until you get in there. Be prepared!

The least you can do here is mentally rehearse the interview itself. Think through the typical questions the interviewer will ask and see, hear and feel yourself answering them confidently. These could be 'Why do you feel you'd be a great sales executive for our company?' or 'What's the most challenging thing you've handled at work, and how did you deal with it?' The next chapter outlines many of the typical questions asked by the interviewer so mentally see, hear and feel yourself answering them well.

Prep 4 – Your image

It never fails to amaze me: the number of scruffy, dirty and inappropriately dressed interviewees that are out there. Believe me, it's not only the grubby that create the wrong impression, there's the teetering-heel brigade who think a six-inch stiletto heel will turn me on, or the guys flashing a bit of chest hair (God, no!). How very wrong some people can be when they think they are dressing to impress!

One of my recent experiences was to interview a guy who turned up in an immaculate suit, only to leave his fly undone with his cartoon boxer shorts on display all the way through the interview. Not my cup of tea, either, girls!

Image isn't just about dress. It is also about the finer details such as your hair, your nails, your teeth, your scent, your body language (more on body language in Chapter 19) and your accessories.

Here are six image checks for interview. Consider rating yourself out of ten for each. Once you have done it, ask someone else who will be honest with you to assess you as well. Do your results agree?

i **Dress Sense** – Your clothes must be neat, pressed well, and, because it is often difficult to tell what the culture of the organisation is, it is best to stay relatively conservative. Wear a suit, usually navy blue, taupe or black. In my eyes there is no such thing as looking too professional. Females may consider a blouse and skirt comfortable and I can agree to this, as long as it looks sharp and professional.

ii **Shoe Sense** – Your shoes must match your outfit, so if you haven't a clue then ask. Make sure they are well polished and shine like you. It's stunning the number of times I have heard people make the comment 'You can always tell a man by his shoes, and the size of them!' Ladies, as I said, please no overly high heels. Make sure that tights and socks also match the shoes and please, gentlemen, no joke socks or ties. They look ridiculous, unless you are applying for a job as a circus clown.

iii **Hair Sense** – Consider getting your hair tidied up and looking sharp in preparation for the interview. Watch the colour of your hair, and if you are male and it is currently in a centre parting or a hippy look I would seek advice immediately if I were you. For those of you who are challenged about what you do if you have too little hair, then just tidy up the bits that remain – and remember, bald guys are said to be very sexy so you have a head start.

iv **Nail Sense** – It may sound daft but believe me, interviewers notice grubby nails and nails that are bitten right down. Get them grown and then trim them down. Make sure they are clean. There's nothing worse than seeing the remains of yesterday's gardening or even worse underneath a nail.

v **Odour Sense** – Smells either create turn-on or turn-off. Fragrances can be worn, but please ensure you don't overdo it. The best bet is to buy a quality one, rather than some cheap tat you got off the market. Body odour is an absolute no-no, so make sure you use a strong odour-free deodorant. And of course do take a bath or shower on the day of the interview. Cleanliness will be part of your divine overall picture.

vi **Teeth and Breath Sense** – If your teeth are decaying or very yellow, then get them fixed now. Bad teeth are so off-putting that a typical interviewer may concentrate on how repulsed she is by them rather than on your ability to do the job. Not only are good teeth important, but so is your breath. Your breath needs to be odour free, so avoid garlic or curry the night before the interview, and never mix drinking coffee with a cigarette: they produce a repulsive combination. If in doubt, get a breath freshener from the chemist.

Prep 5 – The questions to ask

Not only will you be expected to answer questions, you will also be expected to ask them. By asking questions that are relevant, you will seem enthused and genuinely interested in the role. However, avoid asking questions for the sake of it. Ask around three questions as a rule, but if they have been answered during the interview it is perfectly acceptable to explain that to the interviewer.

Here I've outlined ideas for questions you may wish to ask at the end of the interview:

- 👍 What business developments does the department/company have at the moment?
- 👍 Does the company have long-term career opportunities?
- 👍 What would you want to set as my challenge for the first month?
- 👍 How is the department structured? How many people are employed in the department?
- 👍 Does the company have any product development plans at the moment?
- 👍 What are the key locations of the company? Is it possible to relocate during my longer-term career with the company?

Below are questions to *avoid* asking at the interview:-

- 👎 What is the salary?
- 👎 What is the holiday entitlement?
- 👎 Would I get promoted quickly?
- 👎 How long have you been here, and do you plan to stay much longer?

👎 Would I be able to bring my dog to work, as he gets nervous being left alone?

👎 Do you fancy meeting me for a drink some time?

The Preps will help you to plan logically for your interview, and avoid many of the common pitfalls by using your loaf to make sure you look and sound the part. They may seem too much like simple common sense and pointing out the obvious, but believe me, my dears, there's not enough common sense in the world and we all tend to overlook the obvious.

Job Grabber *check list*

- ⭕ Write down and check through a list of the preparations you need to make: e.g. clothes, company research, recap on your CV
- ⭕ Do you feel confident? If not, do some more preparation
- ⭕ Go through the preparation advice
- ⭕ Use your common sense to prepare

Questions, questions – so many questions 17

Your ability to cope with questions – and provide inspiring answers – at an interview will be central to you being offered a new job or a promotion in your current organisation.

The main reason questions are asked is to ascertain if you are up to scratch when it comes to fulfilling the demands and expectations of the role you have been given a chance to win. Don't get on your high horse and think, 'Who the hell are you to ask me probing questions about me and my life?' because that's their job. It's their business at stake, and they want the best person possible to fulfil the role.

To support you in the interview process in what, for many, can be the most challenging part of the job/life progression, I am going to explain the top 100 generic interview questions I have encountered. I will also offer you example answers that will support you in giving convincing, job-winning replies.

In addition to the questions I outline in this chapter, be aware that you will also be asked job-specific questions designed to check out your technical competencies. Be sure to think what job-specific questions you will be asked and plan your answers. Get off your backside and do the research.

The questions that follow are grouped into two key areas, and they are:

- Questions to help understand you – these are the questions the interviewer will ask that will explore your career to date, your attitudes and your personality.
- Questions to explore your specific skills and capabilities – these questions are designed by interviewers to explore whether or not you have the job-specific skills to carry out the role.

When you apply for the new job, think through which of the questions in each category you are most likely to be asked. To determine this, think of which questions you would ask if you were the interviewer interviewing you. You know you best, and you drafted your CV, I hope, so no excuses for not having brilliant answers.

Let's now explore each category and consider the alternative answers suggested. They show that there are different ways to answer each question, and you need to think about the style and delivery that suits you.

Steve Miller

Questions to help the interviewer understand you

1 Tell me a little bit about yourself

I am based in Huddersfield and have a background in the publishing sector which matches closely the requirements of this particular role. I have been described as someone who has a warm personality and I have a results-driven approach to my work. I have many interests and hobbies including travelling extensively and making wine which I enjoy doing in my spare time.

I grew up in Yorkshire, went to university in Scotland, and now live in Huddersfield. My career has been in publishing sales and marketing, so I've got some really relevant experience for the job. I love making deals and making sure my clients are happy with the products they buy and the service I give them. After university I travelled in Asia, going to India, Nepal, China and Thailand, and now, when I have spare time, I make my own wine.

2 Describe to me your career to date

I started my career in holiday entertainment and the reason I started in that field was because it provided a solid base of experience for me to build from. Moving forward I went on to the Rank Group, where I developed further skills, including managing a large business unit and driving customer footfall. My latest role was working at IPC Consumer Media where I have been responsible for managing the HR team.

My first job was as a holiday camp entertainer where I looked after guests, making sure they loved the experience and came back for more. From there I went on to work for two major corporate groups in management roles, and these were the Rank Organisation and IPC Consumer Media. In both these roles I managed teams responsible for adding to the company's bottom line success.

3 Why have you decided to apply for this role?

I have been considering a move for a while as I want to extend my skills base and build on my experience. I am confident that this particular role will do that, because it brings the opportunity to manage a small team and manage the whole production team. In addition, I want to work in this particular sector because the products and service fascinate and interest me. I have done some research on the organisation, and I understand that you are planning to develop a European arm of the business which again interests me because of the opportunities it may bring.

I need a new challenge because I've gone as far as I can with my current company. I really want this job because I know I have the ability to inspire and lead people; I just need the opportunity to demonstrate this. I lived in France for five years and became fluent in French and I know you are planning to expand your European operations with a sales office there and that really excites me, especially if I got the chance to work in this team.

4 Tell me what you know about our organisation

I am aware that your organisation employs 2,000 people and the focus is on providing IT business solutions. The Chief Executive is Harry Smith and I understand the current share price is £11.95. The organisation is now considering expanding into the Far East, to take advantage of the rapidly expanding economies there, and is also opening a sales office in Europe. The product range includes over 200 software packages.

According to *Business Insider* you're the fastest growing provider of bespoke and off-the-shelf e-commerce solutions in the North and have won some major accounts recently, including the Harvey's Furnishings group. The reputation you have is for developing cutting-edge software, and this has attracted a number of clients in China and Japan.

5 What talents do you have for this particular role?

The three key talents that I can bring to this role include being a skilled communicator, problem solver and someone who has a passion for delivering the best customer service possible.

I am excellent at putting customers first and doing my damnedest to make sure they come back again. If they have an issue, I help them quickly and efficiently, and if I can't, I find someone who can. I think I'm really good at dealing with all kinds of people, face-to-face and on the phone.

6 What do you like most about yourself?

What I like most about myself is my ability to create relationships with people. I can communicate with people at all levels and have the natural aptitude to show empathy with people whilst at the same time having a mind of my own. I guess I have an assertive personality that builds trust and respect.

My ability to adapt to situations, work with others and to make sure the job is done to everybody's satisfaction.

7 What parts of your personality do you dislike?

Occasionally I can take too much on and neglect other areas of my life such as family. That said, I have recently managed to learn about building a work–life balance.

I can get too focused on my passions – work and my hobbies – and can ignore other things and other people. I've been working on getting the balance right.

8 How do you cope with working on your own?

I have experience of working alone. For example I remember a time when I was working on a major pitch and it involved many hours being alone so that I could concentrate. I do enjoy working as part of a team, but sometimes there is a need to switch off from others and work independently.

I'm disciplined and focused on the task in hand, but I also enjoy the rapport and support when working within a team.

9 Tell me how you fit into a team.

In my last job I spent most of my time being part of a team. I enjoyed it as we were able to share ideas. I fitted in very well and was often the one who championed team outings such as bowling or theatre trips.

I understand that we are all different people with varying skills, strengths and weaknesses and I work with others to bring out the best in me. I've worked in teams and have been part of a fantastic spirit and drive.

10 What career aspirations do you have?

I do have ambition and I aspire to climb the corporate ladder, managing more people. That said, my priority at the moment is to achieve this particular role and make a great job of it.

One day I'd really like to rise to the top and be on the board, and I think your organisation offers the opportunities for talented people to be nurtured and promoted.

11 Describe your key strengths to me

The first has to be my natural ability to communicate with people. In my last job I was responsible for team briefing and compiling team reports, as well as meeting with my customers on a one-to-one basis. The second is my ability to manage pressure. I have a number of techniques I used in my last job, such as time management tips, and also yoga, which really helps. My third is definitely my perseverance to get the job done on time and completed thoroughly. In my last role, meeting deadlines was crucial and I never missed one.

Inspiring others through clear, direct and sensible leadership. I'd also say I'm a pressure junkie who can take on demanding tasks and get others to support the delivery of brilliant results. I take great pride in delivering beyond expectation, both in the timescales for projects and through customer satisfaction.

12 How would your best friend describe you?

They would describe me as energetic, confident and warm.

As a great friend.

13 What kinds of people frustrate you most?

It has to be people who moan for the sake of moaning. People who fail to act and don't look for solutions to solve problems.

Procrastinating whingers who miss opportunities.

14 Who do you develop relationships with best?

This is an area of strength for me. I have a versatile personality, so I am able to create a rapport with almost anybody. If I had to say who I form relationships with best, it would be those people who listen, are reasonable and like to get things done.

People who are intelligent and open to other views, ideas and opinions.

15 Give me an example of how you have influenced someone else to do something for you

One of my colleagues used to be very lazy and was renowned for doing as little as possible. There was a time we had a piece of work to do that was too much for one person. I remember sitting down with her and explaining that I could do with her support, and it would be a great opportunity to do something together, and when we finished it we could celebrate by sharing a bottle of wine some time. It worked really well and we became good friends.

Once we had been given a major project with a tight deadline and I needed the support of a colleague who was less than willing. I knew that they enjoyed the challenge, but they were worried we'd miss the deadline and they didn't want to put their name to the project.

Basically, I agreed that if they would give 100 per cent support, I would take full responsibility if we missed the deadline – and if we succeeded they would get due credit. We did it and everybody was happy.

16 How would you describe your communication skills?

I would describe myself as an assertive communicator. Listening is really important to me before I offer my opinion. I am also aware of the tone of communication, and always consider this in written communications such as email as well as verbal. Because I am a composed person my communication is always clear and concise.

I think they are well developed both in written and verbal forms, and I also think that people respect me because they know I listen to them and value their views.

17 Describe your areas of weakness to me

I can occasionally take a bit too much on. I am conscious of this now, so always evaluate what I am doing.

In the past I've been a little too keen to impress and taken on too many projects and responsibilities. I know my capabilities a lot more now and don't hesitate to say if I can't handle something.

18 Give me an example of a time when you had to deal with pressure. What did you do?

I remember when we had a new computer system installed for taking customer orders. At the time we were frustrated because, although we had been trained, many of us felt under-confident and frequently made mistakes. I dealt with it by taking my time, not being afraid to ask for help, and constantly reassuring myself that I was learning each time I processed an order.

We'd got a new ordering system and didn't get properly trained on it and this created a lot tension and pressure in the team. I told myself it was a simple learning process and that I wasn't alone, and got the team to support each other until we got much more competent.

19 What motivates you?

As well as earning a decent salary I am motivated by the content of the job itself. This job I have no doubt will motivate me because it is fast paced, deadline driven and involves a good deal of contact with the general public.

A rewarding job. It makes me get out of bed in the morning and look forward to the day ahead.

20 Why are you the person I should appoint to this role?

There are three reasons that you should appoint me. The first is that my experience aligns itself to this particular role. The second is that I will bring you the highest levels of customer service, and the third is that I am incredibly self-motivated.

I have all the experience you need, I'm passionate about looking after customers, and I'll do a lot more than just getting the job done.

21 If I wasn't to appoint you today, why would that be?

It would have to be that my performance in the interview itself did not achieve the standard. However, as you are aware, I do bring the necessary experience and skill set.

I'm not really sure because I feel I've done the best interview I can, and I know I have the skills you want.

22 If you were successful in attaining this role, how long would you expect to remain in it?

It is unusual for me to put a time frame on length of service, but I would imagine up to three years, after which I would see myself ready for a more senior role within the organisation.

As long as you need me in it.

23 What concerns do you have about working for a company like ours?

There are always new challenges when starting a new job, but I think with clear explanation and induction training the challenges will be met well. As long as that is in place there are few concerns.

Nothing. I'm impressed with your care of staff and plans for the future.

24 How do you cope when you are criticised?

Constructive criticism is about personal development. I see it as a good thing and I'm always open to it. It is a way of learning for me.

If I feel criticism isn't justified, then I will discuss it calmly as I am not a defensive kind of person.

None of us is perfect and it's refreshing to hear valid criticism, but if it's not valid then I'll always talk it through with the person who's giving the advice or observation.

25 What kind of leader do you work best for?

I like a leader who is passionate about doing a good job, someone who communicates well with me and who is generally firm, but fair.

Someone who clearly loves what they are doing, who inspires, leads and gives clear direction.

26 How would your referee describe you?

He would describe me as passionate, flexible and someone who likes to get a job done well.

I'd say they would describe me as adaptable, committed and proud of my work.

27 How would your subordinates describe you?

My team have always known the boundaries. I am absolutely certain they would describe me as balanced, straight talking and fair. I have a style that is very empathic, and I like to think I show the balance between being accommodating and democratic as well as being a disciplinarian if needed.

As someone who listens to them, who's fair and approachable. I also think they would say I know where, and how, to draw the line if things are not being done correctly.

28 What does being successful mean to you?

Without a doubt success is about achieving what you set out to do, being resilient so you never give up, and having ambition for other people. Ultimately it is about being a role model for others to follow.

For me it's about being happy at work and home and inspiring those around me.

29 What does a rewarding career mean to you?

Being able to make a difference and meeting the goals I set out for myself and those set by my manager.

I believe that a rewarding career satisfies my passions for working with a great team, having my drive and results acknowledged and looking forward to each day at work.

30 Have you ever faced disciplinary action?

I am pleased to report never.

No [but don't lie if you have!].

31 Where do you expect to be in five years' time?

My plans are to be managing a team in five years' time. I believe I have the personality to motivate and lead a team and would welcome that opportunity.

I aim to be a team leader contributing ideas and inspiring leadership that will take the company forward.

32 What do you look for most in a job?

I like to work in a job where I believe in the products or services of the organisation. I also look for a job that stretches me because I enjoy learning as I work.

Continuous challenge and an organisation I believe in.

33 How would you cope coming back to work after such a long-term career break?

The skills and experience I have gained whilst bringing up my family are plentiful: for example, organising the household and managing on a tight budget. In addition, having worked before I had the children, I developed strong administrative and report writing skills. It is a bit like riding a bike. Once you have the skills they stay with you for ever.

It's going to be steep learning curve, but I've researched what I need to do and I know I can do it, based on the experience I had before raising my family and the challenges I overcame running a home.

34 What kinds of people turn you on?

It has to be people who are go-getters, people with a charisma and influence who achieve by being themselves.

Passionate people who deliver what they promise.

35 What kinds of people turn you off?

People who do nothing to help when needed, and expect others to do everything for them.

People who are not honest and who ride on the coat tails of others.

36 How competitive are you?

Sometimes I am and sometimes I'm not. It really does depend on the situation I face. In this interview, for example, I am competitive because I want to be the most inspirational person you meet.

As much as I need to be. Being overly competitive can be really damaging, but on the other hand, if you're never going to compete, then you may as well stay at home.

37 Do you feel a competitive environment is a good thing?

If it is appropriate and managed well, then yes. For example, I remember in my last job the sales team would often have competitions to see who could sell the most. The manager made it fun and people were rewarded on effort as well as results, so yes, it can be a good thing to help the business.

If the competitive environment is fair and realistic, then I'm all for it.

38 Describe a time when you have used your initiative

Only last week I had to use my initiative on a commercial matter. I had a decision to make on whether to suspend a customer from using our service or keep him on our books. He hadn't paid his invoices for three months, but he was a big spender. I decided to keep him on the books and allow him to continue using our service as he is one of our top spending customers, but at the same time I called him to arrange a face-to-face meeting.

I've just had to handle a delicate situation where a key customer fell behind on settling their invoices. I could have called in our debt recovery team and stopped delivering our service, but instead I called them to see if we could help resolve any issues. They are still our biggest-paying client.

39 What kinds of things frustrate you?

I am occasionally frustrated by the customer service levels in the UK. I think we are poor at delivering world-class customer service and this frustrates me. On a personal level, I get frustrated when there is a lack of resource which can impact on good customer service. However, I have the ability to work within tight budgets, having done so for several years.

People who don't care about customers. Customers pay our salaries so we have to put them first. I also think great customer care has to be properly supported, and if it's not that can be difficult and disappointing.

40 What would you do tomorrow if you had enough money so that you didn't have to work?

It would have to be a round the world trip to enjoy different cultures, but when I returned I would have to work, otherwise I would be bored. I crave stimulation and work gives me that.

Fulfil my dream which is to travel through India to the Himalayas. I'd look out from the top of the world and think about where I could channel my creative talent, so I wasn't bored for the rest of my life.

41 How stable are you?

I would say that the vast majority of the time I am very stable. I think all human beings go through down times, but we have to pick ourselves up and get on with life.

Very stable, but like everyone I've had the odd wobble when life has dished up something bad.

42 Why did you choose not to go to university?

I needed to earn money and knew I would get the opportunity to study either by distance learning or day release. I worked hard and learnt an awful lot by doing the job. I may consider doing a degree one day, but at the moment I am more concerned with learning through experience.

I wanted to experience work as soon as I could. Most of my friends believed that university would open more doors for them, but I knew that I wanted to get a job, and that's what I did. I don't regret it because I think I've got experience from my career that will take me places.

43 What made you decide to go to university?

Having done well in my A levels I had a thirst to learn and felt it was important to move away from home and learn life skills. As well as attaining my degree, I was able to adapt to become an independent adult to prepare me for the world of work.

I got hooked on the research and theories of behavioural psychology at sixth form college and wanted to find out more about what makes us all tick. Not only did I find out a lot more about what makes us who we are, but I also learned how to shape my own thoughts and arguments to deliver convincing points in debates.

44 How hungry are you for success?

I have always been hungry to do a good job and I am confident that my previous employer would agree. To me hunger is also about continuous learning and constant improvement and I am extremely keen on that.

I have a big appetite for success and that's why this job really appeals to me.

45 Do you think I am the kind of person you could work for?

Absolutely, as you appear to be a fair and strong leader. I also perceive you as a results-driven senior manager with similar energy to myself.

In the time I've met you I'd say yes, and I think we've developed a rapport already.

46 What other jobs have you applied for?

At the moment I have two applications in. The other is for a similar business for a similar role. However, the opportunities and specific responsibilities this role would offer are my favoured option.

A couple with similar companies, but I know you are the pioneers in your field and reward talent and I'd love to get this role.

47 How do you ensure you keep yourself up to date?

I regularly read the professional press and attend workshops and training courses to update my knowledge and skills. In addition, I am a member of a professional networking group that offers the opportunity to make contacts and hear regular briefings.

I get electronic news feeds that keep me up to date with your sector, plus I know a few people who already work here and pump them for the latest news and trends.

48 What is the most engaging feature about you?

I consider the key feature about me is my presence. I have received feedback on many occasions that I have a certain charm and can communicate with a wide range of people from all walks of life.

I'd say it's my sincerity and passion which translate into a warm and approachable nature.

49 How emotional are you?

I wouldn't describe myself as emotionless, but equally I am not overly emotional. I demonstrate emotion naturally in response to differing situations, but also know how to control inappropriate emotions.

I'm human and can be touched by situations and events, but I'm also bright enough to know when to keep my emotions in check.

50 What would you describe as your future goals?

I have several goals. The first is to settle into this role and demonstrate my capability to do a really great job. The second is to grow my IT skills even further, so that I can develop websites, and thirdly I have a personal goal which is to go whale watching.

The priority is to get this job and then be an effective member of the team. I'd like to go for a management role as soon as I am able to, and get there by developing my skills with you.

There are a number of different styles that can be used to answer questions and how you respond depends on your personality and confidence. My answers are given in two different ways; the first ones sound rehearsed and I'd expect you to put your own character into the response, so that it doesn't sound too robotic to the interviewer. The latter responses show a slightly more 'off-the-cuff' style, where you have the confidence to think completely on your own feet and answer by drawing on your own experience, whatever the question.

There's no wrong situation or right situation in which to use the answers – you'll know what's needed, depending on the interviewer and the job that you are after.

Questions to help the interviewer check out your specific skills and capabilities

1 How well do you meet deadlines?

In my last role I was responsible for meeting deadlines on a weekly basis, so I am able to bring experience of doing this. In working for my last company for four years I am pleased to say I never missed a deadline.

Very well. It's been part of my daily routine at work for the last four years.

2 Describe your ability to organise others

I consider my ability to organise others as very strong. I always ensure people are clear on what is expected, and I make sure I monitor their progress towards meeting the tasks I set them. I also ensure people understand clearly what they are doing, why they are doing it, and what the expected outcomes are before they move forward.

It's excellent – I start by making sure everyone knows what we want to achieve and what their input has to be. I keep everyone on target and motivated with positive encouragement and regular updates.

3 Describe to me how you would organise yourself in this role

Setting myself monthly and weekly goals would be important, so that I have a strategic focus. I would also set the priorities and identify tasks each day to help achieve them. I would also utilise the skills of my team and delegate tasks that could be handed over to the rest of the team.

I'd look at our company's short- and long-term strategies and plan my own role and responsibilities to identify what I need to achieve with my time. I'd hold a weekly briefing and make sure we are working from the same hymn sheet on a daily basis.

4 What specific skills do you believe this role requires?

The specific skills the role requires have to be the ability to self-motivate when times are tough, strong communication skills to inspire customers and the other is definitely administration skills. All these skills are critical in a fast-paced sales environment.

Strong organisation and communications skills and the ability to cope well with pressure.

5 What challenges do you think this role will bring?

As this would be my first role for 10 years, having had a career break, the key challenge will be getting back into the routine of working again. I am fortunate to have the kind of personality that adjusts very quickly. For example, I moved recently to a new town and my children had to change school. I had to administrate the whole process of the move but I managed it all very thoroughly.

Plenty of challenges, but that's what I need after the challenges I have overcome bringing up my family. The obvious one, if I'm successful in getting the job, is that I'll be learning a lot of new things at once but, believe me, as a parent that doesn't faze me.

6 How would you evaluate your success in this role?

My success in the role will be measured by looking at whether I have met my objectives, and how well I have developed relationships with my colleagues and customers.

It has to be looking at my bottom line contribution. Other than that, it's how well I fitted into the team and what our clients think of me.

7 Describe to me how you manage difficult customers

The first thing would be to ensure you listen carefully to what the customer is concerned about. This is important as the customer needs to feel you are genuinely interested in their issue. Secondly, it is vital to show empathy with the customer so they can see and hear you are genuinely concerned, and finally to agree action about what you will do to resolve the problem for the customer.

Give them my full attention and understand what their concern or complaint is about. It's then crucial that I confirm how we will resolve the issue to their satisfaction and finally that we learn from any mistakes as a team and business.

8 What knowledge do you have about our products?

I have researched your products by looking at your website and visiting your stores. I am aware the products are manufactured in the USA and all are high quality products targeted at customers with high disposable incomes. The products are produced in small volume as the company prides itself on a boutique style service rather than mass market supermarket style.

My knowledge is thorough. I've looked at your online product offer and had brochures mailed to me, so I know what your core ranges are and who buys them. The fact that they are exclusive products really appeals to me.

9 Do you feel over-qualified for this role?

I am very qualified in terms of both my experience and qualifications. However, I want to make it clear that I would not be here today if I didn't really want this particular role. The duties of the role will definitely stimulate my mind, and I am very motivated to demonstrate that I am committed to it.

No, because I do meet your person specification and have some additional skills. By the same token there are areas that I can develop and improve, and that's why the job appeals to me so much.

11 Do you feel under-qualified for this role?

I can imagine I am younger than many other candidates you will interview today who have managed a team. That said, I bring you solid experience of leading a number of projects where I have managed not only people but also resources. I also have considerable job-specific experience, having worked in a marketing role for several years, and have a natural aptitude to create campaigns that are aligned to the company's philosophy.

I have some really relevant experience and some that may not be directly useful right now, but could be very useful in the future. I'm highly motivated to deliver a brilliant service for you and I think that counts for a lot.

11 What specific training will you require to ensure you perform this role competently?

I have thought about this and fortunately in most areas I can bring the necessary capability to carry out this role. The area I would benefit from would be more job-specific, such as understanding the systems and procedures of the business.

I'm comfortable that I have the experience and skills to get to grips with my responsibilities, so I don't think I'll need any specific training when I start. As I develop with the job, then I think I will always look at what training and personal development will improve my skills.

12 What IT skills do you have?

I am well versed in Word, email and PowerPoint. Over the years I have ensured I have kept myself up to date, and if I need to learn a new skill I often go online as I find online learning a straightforward way to pick up the skills quickly.

I'm confident with most major office and administration packages including Word, Outlook and PowerPoint. I've also handled projects using Sage.

13 Describe how you cope with a fast-paced environment

I'm an energetic person and being in a fast-paced workplace suits my personality. In the past, I have worked in a number of fast-paced environments. For example, when I worked at the student bar it was non-stop from 6 p.m. to 2 a.m., especially at the weekends. Also, when I worked for Woolworths at Christmas, the store was frequently very busy so handling a pressured working environment is something that I have plenty of experience of.

I would say I'm well grounded and used to coping with increases in pressure. I've worked in several retail environments which had seasonal sales peaks where all staff were expected to step up and cope with floods of customers. I enjoyed the challenge.

14 This role requires an assertive communication style. What does that mean to you?

Being assertive is the balance between not being too aggressive and too submissive. To do this I would always listen without interrupting, show a high degree of empathy and then explain my point of view. I have a lot of self-control and confidence, so being assertive is my natural style. I have to be like this with customers in my current job, as well as with my kids of course!

It's about getting the job done, making sure I communicate so the team knows what they are doing and why they are doing it. It's also about listening to their views and questions and supporting their achievements and effectiveness with clear leadership.

15 How will you manage the stress that a job like this often brings?

I exercise every day to burn off the stress and this makes me feel great. I also practise relaxation, such as listening to a piece of music or use a technique to help each of my muscles to relax. I find these techniques work really well, especially a good session of aerobic exercise.

I channel the stress into an intelligent approach to make sure goals are achieved on time and to their brief. If I've stored up any stress, it tends to get released on the punch bag that I use at home to keep fit. There's nothing like giving a punch bag a good walloping to get rid of any stress and anger.

16 How would you cope managing a team for the first time?

The experience I bring includes leading small teams of people. For example, out of work I am a member of the local church group and I lead the Bible study every Sunday. This involves me facilitating a group of 12 people. I can utilise this experience in work. For example, I would first develop relationships with each team member, have a one-to-one meeting with each of them, then set the team and individual goals. The team would see that I am a professional leader, but also human. I would also spend time working side-by-side with them, rather than being the traditional stand-off boss. I will want the team to see that I am not a 'just do what I say' type of leader, but I am there to work with them rather than against them. This will be balanced with a firm style when needed.

I have managed people outside the workplace and I'm confident that I can inspire the team and earn their respect quickly. My style is to understand the people in the team, what their core skills and qualities are and channel them in the right direction, while working to improve their all-round skills.

17 How do you think the economy affects our business?

Because the retail industry is governed by consumer confidence, there are a number of variables that will govern the commercial results of the business. For example, if interest rates rise then confidence and spending on consumer goods may fall. This will then reduce spending in the store.

It has an influence because, if money is tight for people, then they will cut down on non-essential spending and may not buy so many of your products.

18 Describe to me how you solve problems

First I ask myself if there is a problem at all. If there is a problem I brainstorm all the options to solve the problem. I then prioritise the best solutions. Once I have done that, I implement what I consider to be the best solution, but will monitor the success of the solution. I also think it is important to evaluate how well you solved the problem, as you learn from this.

I prioritise issues that arise. For example, if it's an issue with a customer, then I'll deal with that there and then, but in another instance it may be a member of staff who wants to change the holiday they have already booked and that isn't as urgent and could possibly wait until I'm dealing with staffing on a particular day.

19 Tell me about the most difficult decision you have had to make in your career

Dismissing one of my team from employment is definitely the most difficult decision I made. The member of staff had many genuine personal problems, and it got to the point that I didn't know from one day to the next if they would be coming into work. In the end, whilst my heart felt for them, I had to dismiss them to protect the business.

I had to sack a colleague who'd worked with me for a long time, but issues arose that made their performance slide. It was my responsibility to review the situation and support them to deal with the issue, but in the end I had to give them notice to leave the company. It was tough, but I knew it was the right decision for the company, and for them in the end as they were able to get away from the pressure and get some professional help.

20 What parts of this job would you dislike most?

I have read through the job description and understand the duties I will perform, and to be absolutely honest there is nothing that stands out that I will dislike. If I had to identify one point, it would be routine administration because I prefer to be out there talking to customers. However, I have such a lot of experience administrating that I am certain that will be fine.

There isn't anything that I dislike; in fact it's the wide variety of functions that appeals to me and how they match my skills set.

21 What parts of this job will you enjoy most?

I really enjoy managing people and seeing them achieve goals. I am a natural coach, so I am really keen to use my skills in this area.

Helping the team to go the extra mile and develop as individuals and as a collective.

22 What knowledge will you bring that helps you perform the job competently?

I have a thorough industry knowledge and recognise the needs of customers. Also, I am professionally qualified, which means I have to keep on top of professional developments, training and trends.

A professionally recognised qualification, continuous personal development and passion to direct my section into making this business grow.

23 How would you manage a member of staff who was not performing?

I would firstly sit down with the employee and find out if there are any underlying issues such as out of work problems. I would also design a coaching plan, so I could develop the employee to perform better. I would ensure the employee was aware I was there to support them, and I would have an open door policy. I would carry out the coaching plan, but after a certain period of time, if this did not turn around the performance, I would invoke the disciplinary procedure because I have to balance the needs of the individual with the needs of the business.

With empathy and sensitivity, but in the end, if we have gone through performance management procedures and they can't improve, then I will follow the disciplinary procedure to remove them.

24 What personality traits do you have that will make you a good leader?

I am a naturally positive person which I believe employees need to see. Also, I am quite visionary and I like to share vision with my team as it is really important people know where they are going. My other trait is that I naturally involve people in work and I think consulting people on key decisions before making one is critical.

I believe I look for the best in people and all situations, and can find positive solutions to deal with most issues. The other strength I have is to be a team player as well as a team leader who leads; but I also listen to the people around me.

25 Describe how you manage your time

I set my priorities before I start work and I always use a 'to do' list. One technique I also use is to cross things off my list as I do them as this gives me a sense of achievement. I also deal with time wasters assertively and do my best to be decisive.

I know what I have to do each day by finishing the day thinking about tomorrow's tasks and how they will be dealt with. I do this by using Outlook to build a list of tasks and timings.

26 How would you prepare a report?

I am often asked to produce reports for the directors of the company. What I firstly do is ensure I have all the information that is required to compile the report. I then work through five core areas, namely terms of reference, findings, conclusions, recommendations and appendices.

I'd look at the style of reports that your organisation produces, see if they can be improved using my own experience and deliver a well-researched, clear and concise document.

27 How would you take minutes at team meetings?

I always take the key points with the action agreed. I then double-check the facts before I allow the agenda to move on. In my current job I take the team meeting minutes for my manager and have done this for the last two years.

I'm lucky because I can use shorthand and I used to minute some very long and complex meetings. Minuting a meeting will not be a problem for me.

28 Describe to me how customer focused you are

I ensure I am totally customer focused. The customer is the focus of the business because that is what drives revenue upward. I always think what extra service can be given to the customer. For example, what I have started doing in the hotel where I am working, when a customer has checked in, is to call them in their room and check that they are happy with the room and ask them if they require any additional items.

We rely on repeat business and recommendation to increase our occupancy rates, so I am totally focused on the guests and their experience in the hotel where I work. I'm proud to have been an employee of the year because of my commitment to providing customers with brilliant service and a positive attitude.

29 Describe to me how commercial you are

I always keep an eye on our competitors. It is important to see what their price structure is and what they are doing in terms of customer service and product development. I have strong commercial awareness; I've had to focus on this because the market is very quiet at the moment and customers don't spend like they used to. If I want to be at the top of my game being commercial is essential.

I know that a company stands and falls from its commercial success, so I'm focused on keeping current clients completely satisfied and working on strategies to develop new business.

30 How would you bring together two employees who are in conflict?

I would deal with this proactively because it isn't fair on the rest of the team and the business. I would first sit down with them individually, to find out what has happened. Once I had done this, I would meet with them together and discuss the matter in a calm and professional way. I would explain to them that we have to agree a way forward together.

I'd find out what the issue was from each party, and then work out a way to resolve the conflict involving them both at the same time so they could provide their input and views. It would have to be addressed quickly, because these problems can begin to impact on the whole team and business quickly.

31 How do you prioritise your work?

When I get into work I write down everything I need to do that day. I then rank them in order of importance. When I have done that, if one of the activities needs a high degree of concentration, I usually do it in the morning because my concentration is far better.

At the end of a week I spend time planning my daily, weekly and longer-term priorities. I write down the tasks and goals and use my palm-top organiser to set out the priorities and deliver reminders for the week and month ahead.

32 What do you think is most important to our customers?

Aftercare service has to be really important to customers because they have spent a lot of money, and also we want them to recommend us to their friends and family. For example, if a customer finds a fault on their purchase we must be seen to deal with this promptly and give the customer the feeling that we really care. I also think customers expect matters to be dealt with quickly, so we need to act with a degree of urgency. That's the best way to retain and build a customer base.

An efficient and friendly purchasing experience followed by great customer care and after-sales. This is what you have a reputation for and it's what has to be protected and developed at all times.

33 How would you keep error rates to a minimum?

In my current job I have managed to reduce the error rate from 3% to 1.5%. I did this by ensuring I planned and paced myself well, and I paid attention to detail and checked my work. When the task was completed, myself and a colleague would do a final check on each other's work.

By working within our deadlines, but never rushing to complete work. This can be achieved by planning the workload and delegating to the most appropriate staff.

34 What would you do if I requested something that was urgent and then my boss did the same?

I would speak to you both and agree which was the priority. However, if you weren't in the office, I would use my initiative and do the one that in my professional opinion was most urgent for the department and the business. I would then explain to you both why I made the decision. I feel making a decision is better than making no decision at all.

I would explain to your boss that you'd already given me a project that you flagged as urgent and ask him which one should take priority.

35 How would you go about holding a professional disciplinary meeting?

I would ensure that a full investigation was undertaken before the disciplinary meeting was held. I would then write to the member of staff advising them of the reason for the disciplinary and their right to be accompanied. In addition, I would enclose the results from the investigation. I would open the disciplinary by explaining the purpose of it, the right to take adjournments and that I would not make a decision until all the facts and circumstances of the case had been considered in full. I would announce my decision based on the reason for the disciplinary and the circumstances. I would explain the right of appeal, how long the warning would remain on the file and any action agreed to train the employee and I would set a review date.

I would use my own knowledge of disciplinary procedures and thoroughly review the company's policy before I started the meeting and delivered my decision and recommendations.

36 Describe to me how you would cope with dismissing someone from employment?

As long as there was a business reason for dismissing the person, then I would be OK handling this. I appreciate that there are times a manager has to dismiss a member of their team.

I would handle the situation with empathy and sensitivity, because no one likes to be forced to leave their job. I would review the case and explain we had followed the correct disciplinary procedures, and that now we had reached the final sanction which is dismissal.

37 What areas of discrimination are unlawful in the workplace?

I am aware it is unlawful to discriminate on the grounds of sex, race, age, religion, disability and sexual orientation. I like to keep myself abreast of employment legislation as I am aware this is changing by the month.

I know that you cannot discriminate in any situation on the grounds of gender, age, race, religion and sexual orientation.

38 What do you consider makes an effective presentation?

I think it is really important to prepare very well. The presentation should be designed to include the presentation objectives, the main body of the presentation and then a conclusion and, if appropriate, recommendations. I see the most important visual aid as the presenter themselves. When I present I like to maintain a steady pace, have open body language and project my voice at a good volume.

Researching the subject and reasons for the presentation very thoroughly is vital because it will give the presenter confidence and show the audience that they are engaged with the subject. Talking clearly and with expression is also important to keep your audience involved and interested.

39 How would you describe your ability to understand business finance?

I am quite capable of reading a profit and loss account, and have years of experience preparing and managing budgets. I am also experienced in forecasting and have attended finance for non-financial managers' training programmes.

During my career I have planned and managed the budgets for small and large projects and part of this required understanding company accounts and financial reports.

40 How would you manage a de-motivated team?

I would get the team together and share my vision for moving forward, how we will achieve goals together and what will be important. I would let them all know that I value their skills, and that we are going to be a high performing team with a great reputation. I'd also agree a number of team incentives such as theatre tickets, champagne and dinners. The team would need to have a tailored coaching plan, so that they had a sense they were being developed, and of course I would have to bring in what I did in my last job which was 'fry up Friday' where I brought in breakfast. We would all sit together and have breakfast before we started work. It was a great way to end the week.

I would be inspirational, let them know they were valued, and agree a plan of action to change their fortunes that would engage them in achieving personal and team goals. My own style is to keep in close contact with all the team and give them the credit when they are achieving and the support they need if they are not up to the mark. We should also consider a system of rewards and promote the talent we have to make sure people stay motivated.

41 Describe to me your experience of managing projects

I have managed projects both in and out of work. For example, I managed the project to implement a new client record system. I ensured that I forward planned what I needed to do and talked to all those it would affect. I also trained all those who would use it. The success of the new system has just been evaluated and it is working really well.

Previously I have worked with board directors to plan and deliver change management projects that were designed to develop a new work ethic. I listened to the goals of the board and carefully considered the commercial needs of the company before planning a strategy to communicate the change plan to staff and develop training tailored to individual needs.

42 How would you ensure you delivered the best levels of customer service?

I would ensure that both I and my team understood that customer service was our top priority. I would hold regular coaching sessions with my team, so that we had a department that was always striving for continuous improvement. I would also meet with a customer focus group to review their experience and ask how we could improve our service even further.

Put into action a customer relations survey involving customers and staff to find out the areas that we are great at and those which have room for improvement. I'd then recommend any appropriate systems to improve customer service and deliver one-to-one training with any staff who needed their customer focus improving.

43 Describe to me how you would negotiate with suppliers to get the best deals

I would always enter negotiations asking for a very low price. I would set my ideal settlement and my fall-back position. It's important not to let the supplier perceive I am desperate for his product because that only gives him the power. Agreeing volume deals is a good way to get a great rate, so I would negotiate to use his service for six months as opposed to three, but make it crystal clear that I demand a good discount.

I'd work out what price we need to buy their product or service at, and be firm in sticking to that budget. I would also seek to get further discounts for long-term, volume orders.

44 What personal standards do you think are needed in this job?

I believe high standards of personal appearance are essential for this role. Image is everything and in business we are judged on it in a split second. What's more, the right attitude is vital in delivering an excellent service in this role. Poor attitudes eventually filter through to customers and that is unacceptable. We have to monitor our attitude and turn it around if we come to work with a poor one.

A smart appearance is important to impress customers and act as a standard for colleagues. I personally also think that we should leave home at home and come to work to do just that. Too many people bring their personal baggage into the workplace and lose sight of why they are there.

45 How would you describe your personal standards?

I have a very positive attitude to my work which I consider is imperative. I also take pride in my work and ensure things are kept well organised and tidy. Looking professional is vital to me, and getting the small details right makes all the difference.

I was in the Royal Marines so my personal standards are second to none. I expect others to be smart and care about how they look and conduct themselves at all times.

46 How accurate are you in completing administrative tasks?

Because I have an eye for detail I am usually 100 per cent accurate in my work. I also like to spot check my work before I finish it. It has often been commented on that I finish work off neatly and, more to the point, thoroughly.

I'm very accurate and I try to ensure it's spot-on by having a colleague check through what I've done.

47 What is the difference between average customer service and brilliant customer service?

Average is when you do the bare minimum for the customer, but brilliant is where you do something that is above expectation. For example, I remember John Lewis calling me to ensure my washing machine had been fitted to my satisfaction and saying that, if I had any problems, to call them. Also, brilliant customer service is when we make sure we thank the customer for their business and look as if we mean it rather than sounding robotic.

The difference is where you get customer feedback when a customer knows that they have been given really great service. That's what I always aim for and it's a truly satisfying part of work.

48 Describe your creative talents to me

I am very good at looking at alternative ways of doing things. For example, last week I had to come up with some creative ideas of how we could increase customer count by introducing new customer incentives. I sat down and thought out of the box and explained to my director that if we introduced a customer incentive scheme, so that customers gained additional products if they signed up with us for 12 months, we would increase our customer count. He agreed, and we have just introduced it. Customers love it and our customer count has increased by 12 per cent to date.

I'd say that I can go left-field to bring solutions to the table that colleagues may not have considered. Recently I suggested a marketing campaign where we sent customers a miniature desk-top organiser in the shape of a shopping trolley with a cover note explaining our company offered 'a single basket' approach. Customer enquiries jumped by 20 per cent.

49 What would you do to build a team?

I would first set team objectives, so that we were all clear on what has to be achieved. I would then hold a team-building day, where we would explore our strengths, weaknesses, opportunities and threats. In the afternoon, I would do something fun and take the team go-karting. Following the day, I would get us all together to discuss what we had done and what we had learnt in terms of what makes a great team. I would encourage each member of the team to commit to an individual action that contributes to making the team successful. I am also aware that my leadership style would be important and I would strive to have a charismatic approach to the team, sharing my passion, engaging all of them as people as well as professionals.

I would take a 'stock-check' on their individual views and aspirations and tailor a development plan for each team member designed to achieve team and company objectives. I'd review and develop this each month.

50 How do you ensure you carry out tasks competently?

I always make sure that I am clear on what I am setting out to do and that I have the capability to do it. If not, then I ask. I work at a steady focused pace so that errors aren't made, and if in doubt I would rather stop halfway through and double check. At the end of completing the task I check my work again and review it, asking myself if there is anything I have added that shouldn't be there or if anything has been omitted.

Firstly I review the brief for each task and identify any areas that I may have any concerns and issues about and make sure they are resolved and I can handle the task/s with confidence.

Now you can see that the range of questions and answers to prepare for an interview is diverse. The questions can seem, on the face of them, to be easy to answer, and for some they are. For example, 'What's your greatest achievement?', if you've completed an expedition down the Amazon river, is relatively easy. However, if you don't think that you've done a great deal, then it's tougher. The secret is preparation – think about the job you are after, and then start to jot down what you think they may ask you. For example, if you want to get a job as a junior account executive in PR, then they will ask you how you communicate with other people and how you cope under pressure and with meeting deadlines. Just think it through before you get to the interview and things will go smoothly.

Job Grabber *check list*

- Accept you will be questioned and that the interviewer might want to probe
- Think of the questions they could ask you
- Look at the Q&As and think about the style you have in answering questions
- Prepare and boost your self-belief

Rapport's much more than a cheap fragrance

18

T o some people the word 'rapport' is a complete mystery because they don't understand what it means, don't have it and don't want it. Let me tell you that rapport means communicating and making a connection with someone else. In this case, being able to create a 'rapport' is essential because it's all about you connecting with the interviewer, and it's also got to be done within the first few seconds, never mind within minutes, of meeting someone.

You might say to yourself, 'But it's impossible to connect with a complete stranger', in this case the interviewer, but that's a shit excuse for poor communication skills. It is absolutely possible to gain a rapport with those with whom we have little in common, and in fact we can create satisfying relationships with anyone.

For me, rapport is a state of empathy, respect and understanding between two or more people, so I will not accept the excuse that rapport with most people is difficult. That's utter nonsense.

Here's my simple guide on how to establish a really good rapport with virtually anyone.

Rapport is divided into three stages; namely, goals, alignment and positive feelings. All successful influencers work hard to create rapport with the people they work with and meet. They show that they have mutual goals with the person with whom they communicate, they establish and maintain non-verbal and to some degree verbal alignment by matching and mirroring the other person; and finally they produce positive feelings in the other person by using a style of communication that inspires rather than bores to death. So, if you feel you are someone who regularly engages with other people but you send them to sleep, you had better follow my advice.

It's important you understand and believe that you have got to sell yourself to an interviewer. I know from bitter experience that there are people out there who couldn't inspire the thirsty to drink water, so follow my advice and get inspirational.

As soon as you meet the interviewer, you are communicating an impression of yourself and what you have to offer. Stay focused because it is impossible not to communicate in a good or bad way and your actions and behaviours will be absorbed in the conscious and unconscious mind of the interviewer.

Your rapport with the interviewer can be so strong that it is possible for you to hypnotise them; conversely it can be so bad that it turns them off and they don't like you from the word go. Hypnotising in this context is about using a style of communication that triggers the emotion of the interviewer, so that you win over their heart as well as their mind.

Steve Miller

Rapport is about being on the interviewer's level. We like to be in conversation with people who are like us, so your goal is to mirror the interviewer's world.

The connection you develop is about ensuring the interviewer can see, feel and hear you giving them your undivided attention, and is also about making them feel special. At the same time, make sure you don't go over the top and start acting as if you're after an Oscar – be true to yourself and let the real character you have shine.

Steps to grab strong rapport

1 Image

- Image will play a key role, so make sure you don't turn up looking like a clown, or as if you're ready to go out clubbing. Make sure you look professional, clean and tidy, and are odour free. No interviewer likes smelly people who will put them off their lunch, so have a good scrub in the morning, spray deodorant under your arms and finish off with some quality fragrance – but don't overdo it and smell like a tart's boudoir. Look at the fine details about yourself, e.g. make sure that your eyebrows are plucked. I can't bear 'Dennis Healey' eyebrows that look as if they are taking off, or, even worse, nasal or ear hair that will make you look pretty repulsive. If this is you, get it sorted.

2 Subliminal suggestion

- As soon as you meet the interviewer, I want you to smile, not only with your mouth but also with your eyes. Eye contact is important as it shows you are interested and confident. So look the interviewer/s in the eyes and show your inner confidence.

- In addition, I want you to think that you are really pleased to meet him/her, and mentally say to yourself what you want the interviewer to think and feel about you. For example, as you shake their hand, use your eyes to look brightly and confidently into theirs, and in your mind say to yourself how well you both get on. Think that they have confidence in you to do a fantastic job and imagine you are already working together. These thought patterns will be subtly picked up by the unconscious mind of the interviewer.

- We 'vibe' people all the time. Think back to a time when you were with someone and there was something you just couldn't put your finger on. Then a few days later you realise it was because that person was a criminal. Or think back to the time you were in a pub and you just knew something was going to kick off, and trouble flared shortly afterwards. The reason for this is that our unconscious mind picks up these sixth sense thoughts. The interviewer will pick up a host of signals from you as you give off your 'vibe', so make sure you are in control, thinking confident and positive thoughts and communicating well.

- The thoughts you carry in your mind will also be transmitted through your body language, so it is important to have positive thoughts about yourself and the person interviewing you.

3 The handshake

- When you shake hands with the interviewer, ensure that your hand isn't plastered with sweat, isn't limp and certainly isn't what I call a bruiser's handshake that will end up crushing the interviewer's hand.
- Whenever I have interviewed someone with a wet lettuce handshake, I have always wanted to run to the bathroom and wash. I feel it gives the impression that the person is holding back and perhaps hiding something.
- And the times someone has grabbed my hand with the force of 'The Incredible Hulk' I have been equally unimpressed. As I look into their eyes I think that they must be so desperate for the job or so insecure that they want to compensate by shaking my hand off.

4 Mirror mirror

- Matching and mirroring the interviewer's non-verbal and verbal communication style is a good way of gaining and maintaining a connection with them. Matching means subtly copying the body language, tonality, pace and words the interviewer uses. When people match each other, what they are unconsciously saying is we are alike, we have similar styles and values. Remember, this has to be done with caution. Match slowly and don't copy exactly because the interviewer may twig what you are doing or think you have gone slightly bonkers. A good way to do this is to use what is known as the two D's: always DELAY your mirror and DILUTE it a little.

- Mirroring the other person is slightly different from matching, in that you become, quite literally, an exact mirror image to the other person. I'm not going to debate the merits of the styles, but I would go for matching if you are not confident about carrying the technique off. If you get mirroring wrong, the interviewer may think you are a bit of a plonker.

- Show that you really listen to what the interviewer is saying and take a genuine interest in them.

- Listen carefully to the words the interviewer says. Match them, but don't overdo it. Again, if you overdo the matching you will end with the interviewer catching on to what you are doing which will result in an instant loss of rapport.

5 Check out the VAK

- All human beings have five senses, namely sight, touch, sound, smell and taste. Externally, we rely on these senses to communicate with the world and internally to communicate with ourselves. When we internalise our world, we usually have a dominant sense that triggers emotions and words. For example you might get a feeling of excitement remembering a live gig you went to, and when you hear the music and singing it sends a shiver down your spine. When we are thinking as well as communicating, we have a preferred way of doing so. Research tells us that human beings normally fit into one of three groups:

a *Visual* – people who prefer to think and recall in pictures

b *Auditory* – people who prefer to think and recall in sounds

c *Kinaesthetic* – people who prefer to think in feelings, emotions, tastes, touch and smell

If you are able to identify the interviewer's preferred method of internal and external communication, then your ability to generate rapport will be even greater. That said, how do you identify if the interviewer is visual, auditory or kinaesthetic? It's done by paying attention to their word choice, eye movement, and posture and speech style. When you have identified the interviewer's preferred style then you can adapt your own to match them.

Let's take a look at different areas to help you identify their preferred style.

i **Words** – the language the interviewer uses will give you a huge clue to how they process information. To illustrate this, if the interviewer processes information in pictures, it is highly likely she is going to communicate with you the same way by using *visual* words and phrases. Examples may include:

'I see that you worked for Barker and Co. for six years.'

'It appears from your CV that you have valuable experience.'

'If you were to see yourself in five years' time, where would you be?'

An *auditory* person would say:

'I hear what you say. It sounds as if you have researched our organisation very thoroughly.'

'I need to talk this though with my director. Leave it with me and I will sound her out.'

'The way you interviewed today was very good. It was music to my ears when you explained you had experience in our sector.'

However, the *kinaesthetic* interviewer would use words such as:

'My intuition tells me that you have had many experiences managing difficult situations.'

'I need to feel that you have the background that this job demands.'

'It really touched a nerve when you said you had experience in managing small teams. I feel that is a real asset as my gut feeling is that those skills will be needed as we expand.'

ii **Eye Movements** – When you are looking at the interviewer's eyes notice whether they tend to look up, across or down. If the interviewer tends to look up then it is likely they are *visual*. If they look ahead or across, then the probability is they are an *auditory* interviewer. If they are looking down, then the likelihood is that the interviewer is kinaesthetic. Most people will follow this pattern. However, please be aware that life isn't always about pigeonholing people, so check it out carefully against their body language pattern and how they talk to you.

iii **Posture** – A *visual* interviewer will sit very upright rather than slouched; an *auditory* interviewer may tilt their head slightly, and occasionally put their hand to ear. Finally, a *kinaesthetic* interviewer will be more relaxed and maybe slightly slouched. If they kick their shoes off, then you know they have a definite kinaesthetic trait.

iv **Speech** – *Visual* interviewers tend to speak rapidly, the *auditory* will use lots of words and the *kinaesthetic* will have a much steadier pace.

Real Life

Mandy

Mandy was a 23-year-old business studies graduate who I worked with on interview techniques using my Get Off Your Arse style. Mandy was bright, very attractive and dressed really well. On the face of it she had all the right basic ingredients to deliver a really good interview, but she lacked that initial spark which creates the rapport right from the start.

I trained her to get into the mind of the interviewer by thinking what she wanted the interviewer to think of her. This included looking into the eyes of the interviewer with a warm smile of both mouth and eyes, and at the same time thinking that Mandy and her interviewer were already working together, that they had a strong relationship and the interviewer had respect for her. This was all carried out in Mandy's mind.

Mandy, who had initially been sceptical about my recommendations, reported that the beginning of the interview felt so right. The rapport felt strong.

Shortly after our sessions, she was offered a role with a large law firm and has since been promoted twice. Obviously Mandy has great ability, but there is no doubt she now also has a real connection to her boss.

Joely

I met Joely when she was 24 and I thought she was the ultimate bore. She looked dull, had little eye contact and had what I'd call a frumpy image.

I took the original call from Joely and she actually sounded OK, but as soon as I met her I recognised that her personal appearance had to be worked on straight away.

She was applying for her first junior management position: leading a small team of academic researchers. Now, I appreciate academics can be slightly removed from the real world, but anyone wanting to lead has to be inspirational and be able to develop that all-important rapport with others.

As soon as Joely sat down with me, I let her know that her style, even for a boffin, was far too boring and that she looked as though she couldn't inspire bees to make honey. Not only did she completely lack sartorial style, but even had a whiff of body odour. She had to be told. I sent her off to see the stylist for an immediate transformation.

Once over her style issues, we now had to work on her rapport skills. They were non-existent. She didn't have much eye contact, had a limp handshake and half the time looked as if she was desperate to play with her doll collection. Yes, that was her hobby.

I encouraged Joely to adopt new success habits, the first being to hold eye contact with people she met and needed to influence. The second was to match body language and smile as she talked. Two weeks later and we had a breakthrough: she smiled, looked miles more attractive (not a bad thing for any interviewee) and appeared professional. She even managed to start matching body language really well.

We agreed that the application process for the new job should be held off for a further month whilst she continued to develop and polish the rapport skills.

I was so delighted when Joely called me in June 2007, three months after we had started working together. She had been appointed manager of a laboratory in Essex. Hallelujah!

Jane

Jane, who was 36, wanted to return to work after a six-year career break.

She was a very well qualified solicitor and had made the effort to keep up to date with developments in employment law which was her specialist field. In terms of competence to perform her desired role, she was very capable.

Jane contacted me, having heard me on BBC radio, and explained that she was confident in an interview, but the first few minutes were always awkward and tense.

I understood that what Jane really wanted was for me to help her with rapport skills so that she could really make the right impression in those first crucial couple of minutes of an interview. She needed to get the rapport as soon as possible, and know she had it, so that she felt comfortable and less tense. She would then find the interview process and conversations flowed much better.

Jane did look a bit frumpy when I met her and, if I'm honest, a bit too fat. She was paying for my help and wanted my 'say it as it is' style, so she got it right between the eyes. She needed to sharpen her outward image with a modern wardrobe and lose a few pounds. It was off to the stylist to be well and truly restyled. Out with the 90's look and into the noughties.

When she looked miles better, we got on with the work and I helped Jane to understand the mirror and match protocol. She was a natural

When we role played identifying the interviewer's preferred style of communication. She managed to discriminate between the visual, auditory and kinaesthetic very quickly, and she's probably the best client I have had to date on that score.

Jane also practised matching body language and boy was she a star at this. She found our four sessions a lot of fun, and I am really pleased to report she was appointed to a new role as an employment lawyer for a well-known law firm a few months later.

You'll now understand exactly what rapport is, what it's all about, and how to achieve it with someone who's interviewing you, or even someone who you want to influence who you haven't met before. Rapport is absolutely vital if you want someone to be eat out of your hand, to like you, to identify with you and to want you. It's not a cheap fragrance you can spray on; you need to work hard at your verbal and non-verbal communication skills to be able to achieve real rapport when you need it the most.

Job Grabber *check list*

- Understand what rapport is
- Don't overact to establish rapport – be as natural as you can
- Follow the step-by-step guide to establishing rapport
- Identify your interviewer's style and match it

Body
be aware

19

When it comes to making that killer impression at your interview, the eyes definitely have it. Research tells us that around 55 per cent of communication is through body language, so it is hugely important to work on this and get it right. You don't get a second chance to make a first impression, so make damned sure you get it right first time, or you'll have to live with the regret.

The way that we communicate with our bodies is strongly influenced by the way we stand, sit and move our limbs, hands and eyes. Through our bodies we illustrate externally to others our inner emotions and intentions, and so it is essential that we understand and control exactly what our body is saying.

Let's not forget that body language isn't just about your appearance – although, as you already know, it is imperative you get that right, especially if you are a scruffy bugger – but it is also about the way you stand, sit, use gestures and use appropriate eye contact etc.

Have you ever considered how expressive your body is? If not, now is the time. It will be speaking volumes about you at the interview. You will either excite or dampen the interest of the interviewer. It's a bit like when you go on a blind date. You walk in the room, have a look at the guy and within minutes either feel that you could give him a damn good snog or want to run like the clappers. I've legged it from a date myself in the past, so I know what I'm talking about!

Seeing is believing

Have you ever been in a situation where someone has told you one thing, but their body tells you another? For example, I remember asking someone at interview if they managed small projects well. Whilst the verbal reply was 'Yes, very well, as I have had experience of this many times', the body told me otherwise. His eyes were looking more at my crutch area, his hands trembled slightly and as he said the word 'Yes' his head movement was in fact saying 'No'. You've got to admit that seeing is believing.

It is in cases like this that we don't believe the interviewee: not always because of what they say but because of the non-verbal signals which we pick up and then process unconsciously. Body language, in other words, works as a hypnotic trigger, and a powerful one at that. Think about politicians, TV presenters and top entrepreneurs. They spend so much money on their image because it supports their positive use of body language. They need to get it right so that you trust them, are inspired by them and, most of all, believe them.

To influence the interviewer, you must ensure your body language is smart because the most dominant sense is visual with nerve paths from the eye to the brain, so your body language is vital. They will notice the way that you walk into the room; if you look at them, do you smile at them; is the way you hold up your body strong or defensive? You will give visual signals about what kind of person you are from the word go.

To 'hypnotise' the interviewer with your body language, you must exert what is known in the business as 'congruence', or, in other words, your body must say the same as your words. Imagine a groom at a wedding who stands up and welcomes the guests. He welcomes them by saying how pleased he is to see everyone, yet he fails to smile, hops from one foot to the other and has a jaw that is set. Is he really saying he is pleased to see everyone? Now consider the interviewee who explains he is confident enough to organise other people, yet barely opens his mouth when he speaks, looks out of the window as he talks to the interviewer and plays with the ring on his finger. Is the interviewer really going to conclude the interviewee is confident? I doubt it very much. The interviewer's unconscious mind will conclude that he is shaky and cannot be trusted to organise other people.

One final point, and it's an important one so take note. Your body represents your inner thoughts, not only about the interviewer but also about yourself. In the trade this is called 'body manifestation' of 'internal response'. Put simply, your mind will control all your behaviour. That is why learning to relax about yourself, as well as grooming your self-belief, is crucial. If you don't think you have got enough of this just yet, then skip back to Chapter 6 and practise more self-belief exercises.

I want you to be keenly aware of the parts of body language that have to be spot-on for the interviewer, so that you engage the interviewer's interest and emotion. Let's take a look.

Body parts

i Posture

Take a moment to consider your posture right now. If an observer looked at you, what would they be able to read from the way you are sitting, standing, leaning or lying at this very moment? Would it be a good or bad impression? Would they say you are engrossed, relaxed, tired, bored, anxious, cynical, in pain, happy, confident?

I'll bet that as soon as I asked you to become aware of your posture, you started to adjust it, becoming instantly self-conscious of your body. The fact is, we don't really pay much attention to this aspect of our body, as we adjust posture automatically without thinking about it, but to be spot-on at interview you have got to make a conscious effort to get it right.

From this moment on, when you go for an interview, you will pay attention to your posture and be aware of what position you are in and what it is saying about you. A confident, appropriate posture and effective movement can be learnt, absorbed and eventually become second nature to you.

By learning to relax and boost your belief about yourself as described in Chapter 6, you have already gone some way to helping improve posture. Having a calm state of mind and strong belief in yourself will mean you can hold yourself with ease. It will allow your body to move in a manner that oozes vibrancy and in a manner that is congruent with what you are verbally communicating to the interviewer. Body and mind will work in unison to present your inner and outer confidence.

An easy way to develop your posture is to watch other people. Look at how they stand, sit, walk and relax in different situations and environments. Ask yourself what response their posture stirs in you. For example, do you perceive them as confident, professional, sharp, and inspirational? Or do you perceive them as the kind of person you could watch as a cure for insomnia: dull, boring andgrey?

To help build your confident posture try out these posture styles:

- keep your head up, don't look at the floor
- relax your shoulders, don't hunch them
- sit up straight, don't loll
- walk tall, don't slouch

Then do the reverse, then do them again correctly. Feel the difference?

A good way to practise posture movement is to walk around the room shuffling your feet. Now change so that you feel you are gliding, like a model on a catwalk, my darlings! Imagine walking down the red carpet into a Hollywood film premiere. Now change posture and creep around the room; now once again walk tall, stride out confidently. Hold those shoulders high and walk proudly.

Now try sitting in different ways – on the edge of your seat; with your legs crossed; with your legs stretched out; taking up as much space as you can; taking up as little space as you can.

I think an ideal posture for interview is to have the legs crossed neatly at the ankles, pulled in slightly, rather than pushed out, with knees together. Never sit with your knees wide apart, but do relax. You should sit up straight but not stiffly and project your presence just as well as if you were walking tall. You will deliver the same effect, so practise this in your chair.

Now we'll use your biggest muscle – no not that one, guys – the power of your brain to support good posture. Imagine meeting the interviewer for the first time. See, hear and feel yourself using a positive, upright yet relaxed posture. Now repeat this exercise but imagine you are the interviewer – see the candidate approaching you. First see them with a sloppy, hunched posture, slightly tense, and ask yourself how you feel. I guess you feel uninspired, disappointed, probably thinking of how the fuck am I going to spend an hour interviewing this! Now see them as upright, relaxed, fluid and posture confident. Your thoughts change instantly. You may think this could be the one, or you may even have a few naughty thoughts of what you might do with them if this was not in a professional setting!

Posture, along with movement, can inspire professional trust. However, if you get it wrong and look as if you lack confidence, moving in a way that is wooden, then you are much less likely to grab the new job.

If you feel you need to work on this, get practising now. Doing nothing means you remain dull. Get off your arse and practise!

ii Gestures

When we communicate in writing, we sometimes choose to emphasise and stress words and phrases by underlining them or printing them in bold, colours or italics. Gestures can help serve the same purpose.

There is a complex range of gestures that we can use to convey different emotions and to emphasise things we are saying and show that we are confident. You can use a nod of the head, move your hands to express dynamism and movement, and smile or work your eyes to ooze confidence. These can all add colour and depth of meaning to what you have to say to the interviewer, and they can also help you make your case more effectively, more persuasively and more sincerely.

At the interview you need to use your gestures to work for you by getting them to reinforce your verbal messages. For example, if you shake your head whilst saying 'Yes', what are you actually communicating? Your hypnotic suggestion here is most likely to come from the gesture movement – to the interviewer you are actually saying 'No'. Why? Well, remember that the most subtle communication is through your body language. In this case, it worked against your verbal message. You should have nodded as you said 'Yes'.

Another important thing about gestures is that they should have a purpose and they should be associated closely with the purpose and content of your verbal expression. Don't make gestures simply for the sake of making gestures, make them because they help you communicate to the interviewer what it is you intend to communicate. Busy gestures will only mean that you look as if you have taken speed: not a good idea and something I will not tolerate. I don't want you coming across like Adolf Hitler whose body language and gesticulations were as scary as his mind and actions.

Now, let's look together at how you can employ gestures to your advantage in an interview situation. Take for instance the interviewer asking you what you can bring to the role and you respond by explaining that you have valuable experience that can help *increase revenue* for the company. It is on the words *increase revenue* that you slightly raise your right or left arm, palm up, indicating an upward progress. Your visual communication in this case reinforces the content of your verbal message powerfully, and underlines its impact. This is known as a double blind. In effect you are communicating twice. Once from the mouth and once from the body, yet both at the same time.

Now, imagine the interviewer asking what key strength you can bring to the job and you reply, 'Based on my experience I have a natural aptitude to develop strong relationships with both customers and colleagues.' As you say this, your smile and occasional nod of the head will support the verbal communication. Your body here is congruent with the words. You smile because you mention 'strong relationships' and you nod to transfer the message that this is so true about you. In other words, your nodding gesture is hypnotically sending the message to the unconscious mind of the interviewer that this is true.

In another scenario, you are saying to the interviewer, 'In my last job I was able to meet my objectives year on year. In moving forward I want to be able to use this achievement to lead from the front, develop a team of people and exceed targets.' Reinforcing accompanying gestures could be on the words 'year on year' by rolling the left or right hand slowly in circular movements, and also on the words 'lead from the front' where the left or right hand moves out from the body in a gently rising motion. Each of these gestures would support what you said verbally; they all underscore the words.

By focusing on this aspect of your body language, you will also become aware of inappropriate gestures that don't help your cause in the interview. For example, fiddling with a necklace or lapel, moving your wedding ring up and down the finger, or tugging your ear lobe.

Other common pitfall gestures to avoid include crossing your arms in the interview, or rubbing your nostrils or eyes. Can you imagine the unfavourable impression this will give to the interviewer? And avoid holding on to the chair as if ready for take off! Remember to sit comfortably back when seated, but in an upright posture. If you sit on the edge of the seat it will create an impression of nervousness and lack of confidence – or it might suggest that you don't want to be there at all, so the interviewer will begin to feel they themselves are not valued and that you are more interested in rushing off to do something different. Finally, avoid hands behind the head. Not only will this make the interviewer feel uncomfortable, but such a gesture can make you out to be a cocky little sod who needs a kick up the arse!

Be aware of your body movement, and practise gesticulating in front of a mirror to help spice up your impact. It's really worth doing because your gestures will become more natural the more you practise. You should also try practising gestures when engaged in conversation with friends, to gauge their reaction and feedback. Remember not to allow your gestures to get too busy or too emphatic, otherwise your interviewer/s will think they are at amateur dramatics.

iii Facial expressions including eye contact
As with gestures, it is really important that your facial expressions back up your verbal communication and emotional intentions.

You already know the power of the eyes in building rapport, and what we'll do now is not only review the impact of the eyes, but also your other facial expressions.

I want you to practise relaxation. This will help you to express yourself more naturally through your face. If your facial muscles are tense, this will communicate itself to the interviewer and impede your flow of communication with them. It makes it more difficult to smile with both your face *and* your eyes – something you need to be able to do to inspire confidence and create rapport.

Your eye contact and minute facial movements are crucial to communicating well. No doubt you will have heard the expression that the eyes are the windows to the soul. It's true that the eyes communicate so much about you, and that you can form a connection with another person with eye contact alone.

Avoiding eye contact will communicate a lack of confidence in you, but worse still you may come across as a bit shifty, insincere and untrustworthy. If you find eye contact a bit difficult, then try looking at the bridge of the other person's nose, because if you do this you will still appear to be giving them eye contact. Eventually you will become more confident and eye contact will happen quite naturally.

As Chapter 18 mentions, it is crucial to smile with your eyes to create rapport with the interviewer. You also know you can hypnotise the interviewer with your eyes. This is done by simply channelling your thoughts through your eyes. As soon as you meet the interviewer, imagine the conversation you are having is pleasurable. Think positively about the interviewer as well as yourself. By looking at the interviewer and really seeing them as a person as well as a professional, you will make them feel acknowledged. Not only that, but your inner thoughts will affect the impact of the eye contact. Any negative thoughts about yourself or the interviewer will be transmitted through this 'invisible' yet powerful connection, so think positively about the interviewer at all times. If you do this, it is so much more likely that they will think positively about *you* and seriously consider you for the new job.

Real Life

Diane

Diane was a 30-year-old police officer who was ambitious and wanted to move onwards and upwards in the job through the force's career structure. She applied for the position of sergeant and was offered an interview, but was terrified at the prospect of the process and the panel interviews that she would have to go through.

She came to see me and talked about her high levels of anxiety when it came to even thinking about the prospects of presenting her case for promotion to the interview panel and attending an assessment centre.

On the really positive side, Diane had a terrific amount of experience, and on paper was a really hot candidate to get the promotion. She talked with oodles of confidence about sailing through the sergeant's written exam.

However, having met her, I could see that she struggled with eye contact with people, especially those in a position of authority and she knew that if she became a sergeant she would have to deal with senior colleagues a lot more. The eye contact thing was a real shame because she has the most gorgeous large brown eyes, and to be honest, people would pay to have her cast a glance at them.

The block to getting effective eye contact at the assessment centre would really prejudice her chances of landing the promotion that she desperately wanted, but the more she thought of this block the more Diane was petrified of looking the interview panel members in the eye. I knew she'd had no trouble with the criminals she'd come across in the role as police officer — she had a good record of arrests — but it was the senior officers she'd have to win over at a promotion board that would be the problem. It would truly be a crime if she couldn't get over this block to get where she should be.

To get her into shape for the challenge of promotion, I really jacked up Diane's self-belief before practising eye contact. Initially I got Diane to look at the bridge of the nose, which takes the edge off for people who aren't yet comfortable with eye-to-eye contact.

I set her a task: to arrange to go and visit people who she believed were authority figures, so she could practise maintaining eye contact. These included people such as her bank manager to discuss her savings, the local MP where she would discuss her concerns on law and order policy, and finally the doctor to request a medical. Over several weeks she practised and practised until the complete eye contact habit was achieved — no longer looking at the feet or the bridge of the nose.

Diane came back to me shortly after our work together and told me she'd attended the assessment centre and achieved the role of sergeant, and that the interview panel were impressed by her sincerity. Two years on, and she is now applying for the role of inspector. She reports her eye contact is brilliant and she has also used it on Saturday nights when out with the girls, clubbing. Go girl!

Sarah

If there was a medal for defensive body language, this girl would have won it. Sarah was a 26-year-old care worker who came to see me to help increase her impact at job interviews.

She had a certain charm about her and was dressed immaculately, but her body language was so off-putting. Whilst our conversation was light and everyday she was fine, but as soon as there was a move into a more professional dialogue her eyes opened as wide as saucers and her body language became tense to the point I thought she was going to explode. Her arms were tight into her body, obviously protecting her from a perceived threat.

Quite clearly Sarah was not as confident as she made out, and she couldn't handle the rapport between two people when the stakes were raised. I knew that she needed to relax about herself and increase her self-esteem.

For the first couple of weeks I decided to help her to dramatically increase her self-belief by doing some self-belief exercises, both with me and at home. After this, we were able to work on getting her to release and relax her tight posture. The first step was to get Sarah to allow herself to have her arms open as we talked, at the same time breathing deeply as she looked into my eyes. After she had practised that, I then posed some interview style questions to her, at the same time getting her to maintain the relaxed open posture and eye contact.

Over the next two weeks, I asked Sarah to practise the 'inspiring interview technique' to reinforce her new open and relaxed style. She successfully began to take on the more positive body language and felt more confident and equipped to apply for supervisory roles in a number of care homes.

Three months on, she applied for a job at a care home where she really wanted to work. She attended two interviews and was appointed to the role.

Joanne

A 36-year-old mum aiming to return to work after bringing up her gorgeous twins, Joanne had worked as a personal assistant and wanted to return to a similar role. Having been out of work for the last eight years, she was not only nervous about returning to work but also the interview process.

Her CV showed she was well qualified, and to back it up she had a very pleasant personality. There was no doubt she had a strong image, but she had a few inappropriate body language problems.

As we practised the interview setting, she would play with the rings on her finger, hold her ear lobe at intermittent times, and worst of all, her neck would go incredibly red and blotchy.

We agreed a polo neck top could help cover up these blemishes, but Joanne was not at all comfortable wearing them. As we chatted, it was obvious that Joanne's internal thoughts about herself had been shattered. Not only was she struggling to bring up the twins, and needed to return to work to be able to look after them, but her husband had gone off with a woman 10 years younger than Joanne. As the story continued, it was evident that she had suffered many put-downs from this rat and, to be honest, he deserved the same fate as any other vermin.

We eventually moved on and Joanne worked on some self-belief exercises. She affirmed her belief in herself and reconnected with her self-worth. This bastard had done his best to destroy her, but little did he know that I was far stronger than he.

After four weeks of building her belief structures, Joanne was becoming a different person. She looked more radiant, attractive, more at ease and, yes, when we practised the interview sessions she was relaxing her posture, sitting up straight, leaving the ear lobes well alone, and as for the wedding ring – it was gone! She was starting a new life, and grabbing a new job would be part of it.

A month later Joanne was appointed as personal assistant to a finance director in a large multi-national business. I hear from her from time to time and can tell you that this member of the Get Off Your Arse army is happily married again, this time to a soldier. Lucky girl!

I know you can now appreciate that presenting your body positively – as a package of your posture, facial movements, your eyes and gestures – is as important as having your mind focused on being in that new job. The two connect, so that you become irresistible to your interviewer and they can't have anyone else in the job that's on offer.

Steve Miller

Just remember that body language is a positive tool if you have command of it, but if you don't have control at an interview it will sink you faster than the *Titanic*. Remember to breathe deeply and use your brain to keep all the positive eye contact and correct posture going well. Go knock 'em dead!

Job Grabber *check list*

- Be aware of the impact of your appearance and body posture
- Use expressive body language, but don't go OTT
- Get your emotions and thoughts in check as they will be evident in your face and body
- Use your body to be positive and influence the interviewer

From boredom
to boardroom
– your voice,
your words

20

Most interviewers will gauge a lot about you from the quality of your voice, so you need to be able to project it correctly and make sure it scores maximum impact. Your ability to relax and be relaxed about yourself in the interview situation will play an important role in the quality of your voice production.

If you are tense, your voice will suffer as its output and ability to project words effectively will become restricted and you will not be able to make the most of this key tool in your communication with the interviewer. The problem will show itself in a shaky voice that won't project the confidence that you must get across.

Muscular tension restricts the abilities of your chest muscles, your diaphragm and your facial muscles, and this will affect the quality of the sounds that come out of your mouth. In fact, tension in any part of your body can have a negative effect on your voice, so if you tend to suffer from tight shoulders and stiff back try to get someone to give you a massage or maybe have a warm bath before you go to the interview to release any muscle tension.

A good way to put the power of your voice into context is to see your body as a musical instrument, say for example as an acoustic guitar. The tone, volume and quality of sound produced by a guitar can be hindered if the body of the instrument is flawed in any way. The same goes for you, so pay attention to getting your body in tip-top shape.

Everyone can have a great voice that is capable of expressiveness, and your voice will play a major part in shaping the interviewer's judgement of you. So think about the following:

- How good a voice have you got? How flexible, powerful and versatile is it?
- Can you use your voice to produce a mood, a reaction, excite an emotion?
- Are you really making the most of this asset?

I'm not talking about having a big gob (there's only room for a few of us!); it is about using the melody and tonal qualities of your voice to best effect.

To make the most of your vocal equipment it pays to exercise it. The muscles we use to produce sounds are no different from any other muscles in the body. If we don't keep them in good condition, if we don't use them to their full extent, they become flabby, ineffectual and can't do the job they were designed for. Well, they still do a job of sorts – we can still speak and make ourselves understood – but we have no control over them, we find they will not respond in the ways we want when we need them to. For example, if you're in a meeting and want to make a point, but you are nervous when you speak, the chances are the tone and melody will be all over the place and people are not likely to be convinced by what you are trying to say to them. They will think you are insignificant and be dismissive of you.

In the interview your voice tonality has to be confident, warm, and firm. If it comes out thin and lacking power and conviction, maybe in a dull monotone, you are likely to send the interviewer to sleep. You'll be forgotten as soon as he/she kicks your arse out of the interview room and they look forward to meeting the next candidate.

The words you choose to use are another important tool that has to be carefully considered. Whilst statistically words account for only around 7 per cent of the communication we make, don't be fooled. In terms of impact I'd say that words will make 70 per cent of the positive impression that you want to give compared to the 25 per cent that body language can convey. As you progress through the interview your choice of words will become ever more important. 'Power words', or positive words are useful in creating a lasting impression. In this chapter you will understand what kind of power words to use and, more importantly, how to use them.

Voice exercises

So, it is time to exercise your voice so that we make it clear, concise, inspiring and of course engaging. Have a go at these. Don't worry if you feel like a bit of a prat. Well, I'm sure you will look like one, but, hey, no one is going to see you, so bollocks to anyone else, just get on with it.

Steve Miller

Exercise 1

i Relax by tightening all your muscles, holding them taut for five seconds and then releasing them; do this three times and enjoy the waves of relaxation you feel. Take a few deep breaths, filling your lungs from the bottom up; try to avoid breathing shallowly when only the upper part of your lungs is being used. You can identify when you are breathing with more of your lung capacity because you see your stomach rise before your chest does.

ii Now place your fingertips at the bottom of your ribcage and laugh and/or cough – although laughing is preferable as it realises positive emotions. What you will feel is your diaphragm working the muscle that aches when you laugh yourself silly.

iii Now, as you breathe out, hum a mid-range note. Where can you feel this note in your body? In your chest, throat and stomach? Repeat the exercise, but this time hum a high note and again feel where the note vibrates in your body. Perhaps the note is higher, possibly in your face, or at the top of your head.

iv Repeat once again with a low note. Maybe you feel this note lower in your gut or maybe in your feet. Go on, be a drama queen! Now imagine that your note is on an escalator inside your body. It starts high, on the top floor, and moves down through mid-range to low until it is in the basement and then back up high to the top floor again.

Don't get any smart ideas, like you think I'm training you to be in a choir. You need to get your voice in shape and, whatever it takes, I am going to get you there.

Now, what else can you do? Oh yes, there is more! Here we go, let's try this. Again you may feel a bit of an idiot, but it is in your interest, so get on with it.

Exercise 2

If you felt a bit of a drip in the first one, then you might well feel it again in this, but don't worry. Oh well, if you look daft, so be it. You've got to do it and that's that.

This exercise will show you that you have much more capacity in your voice than you may have ever believed. First of all, say a few lines out loud, something simple like a nursery rhyme. Now, stand with your feet comfortably apart and flop forwards from your waist like a rag doll.

Next, begin to swing your arms from side to side like a monkey. On each down swing, breathe out audibly and say **'huh!'** Get a good rhythm going, but you needn't do this for too long. Try about ten 'huhs'. I now need you to stand up straight and repeat your nursery rhyme.

Many people find that this simple exercise frees their voice and they acquire power and volume without strain or effort. I'd advise that you do this on the morning of the interview and be assured it will help strengthen the power of your voice.

Exercise 3

Sometimes our voices are less effective than they could be as we don't articulate our words clearly. Imagine slurring your words at interview, cutting the ends off words and generally not forming your words properly. Not good, is it? To assist this aspect of your speech at the interview it will help to give your facial muscles a decent work out.

Try out some of the following favourites:

i Mime chewing bubble gum and then blowing a huge bubble.
ii Blow raspberries.
iii Try to touch the tip of your nose and then your chin with your tongue. Whether you do or not makes no odds.
iv Smile as widely as you can, purse your lips, and smile again.
v Try saying a tongue twister like 'red lorry yellow lorry' at a reasonable pace and then speed it up, concentrating on getting the words formed correctly.

Consider for a moment the importance of having well-conditioned vocal equipment and exactly how this will help you deliver the best of you at your job interview. The melody of your voice will help or hinder your demonstration of a sense of conviction and belief in yourself. Remember, you are the product and you need to sound confident, interesting and excited when appropriate as you sell yourself. The rhythm of your voice will contribute to the final outcome of whether you are offered the new job. When you are in control of your voice you will be able to respond to the interviewer with ease and you will be able to find the appropriate melody to communicate your intentions. For example, if you want to demonstrate confidence you will sound slightly firmer, and if you want to demonstrate compassion you will sound a little lighter.

Emphasis and timing

Pauses will be an important part of your speech at the interview. They help break up what you have to say into manageable parts, and emphasise particular points and issues. Speech that trundles on without pauses can be hard for a listener to follow, and can easily become meaningless and boring.

The pauses you use are your great hypnotic allies. They do more than simply organise the content of speech. They can help create the mood and emotion you want to trigger in the mind of the interviewer.

They can be used to draw the interviewer into what you say, to grab their interest, align their emotions with your own and keep things completely positive. Pauses will create confidence and excitement, and can provoke thought as well as stressing and underlining aspects of what you want to say.

Emphasis, pace and timing work together to create fantastic effects when it comes to delivering your words during an interview. Let's look at how emphasising words slightly will make you sound more interesting. Also, a slight emphasis on a word will ensure that word enters the unconscious mind of the interviewer. This again is based on the principles of hypnotism, in that the unconscious mind will tend to remember these words as they are different from the other hundreds that you spout out.

When words are emphasised there is a different melody to the communication. The word you emphasise gets registered more strongly than the rest of your communication, so it is useful to consider which words you want to plant in the mind of the interviewer. In other words, I'm helping you to make things stick in his/her long-term memory.

These words that you plant in the long-term memory of the interviewer will be what the interviewer associates with *you*, so it is vital that you choose them carefully. Whenever I train someone to hypnotise the interviewer, I encourage them to use a maximum of three 'power words'. These words are positive and will not only encourage the interviewer to associate you with them, but they will trigger a positive emotion in the interviewer's psyche.

The list below sets down some of the ass-kicking power words that I tend to use in conversations where I want to see a result that comes out my way.

Power words

Inspire	Sharp	Result
Maximise	Inject	Deliver
Climax	Explosive	Expedient
Accelerate	Driven	Build
Optimise	Increase	Opportunity
Double	Inspirational	Strong
Impact	Invest	Effective

The list could go on and on. Have a look at the above, but do try to think of some of your own that you are comfortable with. Now, let's consider how and when to place a power word. These are the key stages:

i Construct your sentence
ii Pause slightly before saying the power word
iii Emphasise the power word slightly

In conversation with the interviewer ensure the power word is spoken at least three times. The first time is the time the word is registered, the second time the word is reinforced and the third time they own it.

Of course, you can't be certain what the interviewer is going to ask you, but for all interviews you can construct a few sentences that you can say during your job pitch. You know what job you are applying for, and you know you have to sell yourself in the interview, so a little common sense tells us what might be asked. For example, if being interviewed for a first line management position, it is likely you will be asked about your management and leadership style. If applying for a personal assistant position, it is likely you will be asked how you organise yourself; and if you are applying for a business strategist position, it is likely you will be asked how you project manage.

Let's look at several examples here. I bet your bottom dollar it would be possible to say the following sentences during the interview:

1 Interview for a first line management role

'I believe one of the key qualities of the modern day leader is to ensure that they are self-aware so that they [slight pause] *inspire* their team.'

Here *inspire* is slightly emphasised so that the interviewer's mind registers that word. As the interview progresses, you would say that word a couple more times after a subtle pause, so that you can be more certain the interviewer's mind really begins to associate you with the word *inspire*.

2   Interview for a personal assistant's position

'Over the years I have learnt many ways to ensure I manage my workload. I have made sure that I manage my time so that I am really, really [subtle pause] *organised.'*

Again you would drop the word a couple more times into the conversation with the interviewer so that his/her mind associates you with a person who is *organised.*

3   Interview for the position of business strategist

'Over the years I have *managed* many *projects.* I have always ensured I set SMART objectives for the projects, identified the resources required, set out the tactical actions to achieve the objectives and finally evaluated the success of the project. In doing so my skills to [subtle pause] *manage projects* have been professionally developed.'

You could then go on to give the interviewer specific examples of projects you have managed and again reinforce the words *manage projects.* When you leave the interview room the interviewer will certainly be confident you can manage projects.

Just to recap. You now understand the power of your words, that using the instrument that is your voice to its fullest capacity is essential to unlocking the door to a successful job interview. There should be no doubt in your mind, whatever the job you want to grab, that your voice can and will 'charm the pants off' the interviewer if you get it on the money. So spend some time and do the 'daft' exercises I've set out, and you will go from 'boredom' to 'boardroom' if you want it.

Job Grabber *check list*

- Get to know your voice
- Practise the relaxation and voice exercises
- Be aware of the tone of your voice and the words you choose to use
- Know your 'power words'
- Your voice is a great instrument, so practise with it and use it to its greatest effect

Panel interviews

21

Many of you will be shit scared when it comes to being interviewed by one person, but just imagine if you have to face two or three people in a panel interview. You could well turn into a jabbering wreck, unable to communicate how good you really are, and that would be a complete waste of time for you and them.

I'm going to set out a range of tips and secrets that will help you to feel relaxed about facing a panel interview, and help you to get through it and shine.

The panel interview may be used at the second stage of the selection process, and is likely to be more detailed and probing than a one-to-one. The questions asked may refer back to your first interview, to assessment-centre activities or even aptitude tests.

Never assume that your interviewers are familiar with the answers you gave at the first interview, and don't assume how many people will interview you. In fact, don't be surprised to see more than three people if you are applying for a senior role in the public sector.

Many people dread these sorts of interviews and find them a bit exhausting to say the least, but I want you to see them as a great opportunity to impress an audience with you as the star.

Panel in pieces

There are a range of issues and challenges that the panel interview throws up for the interviewee. The lack of opportunity to interact with everyone in the room is often a problem, but I will help you overcome this.

Depending on the panel, one person may ask all the questions, but even if the entire panel takes it in turn to talk to you, you will most probably find yourself drawn towards talking to one person more than the others. This could be for any number of reasons: perhaps you establish great eye contact with them, get them to smile, or maybe they understand where you are coming from straight away.

That said, everyone on the panel will have a say as to whether or not you get the job, so it's essential that you treat each person with the same level of respect and importance. If there is one you don't like, it's simple – pretend you do!

I am going to tell you how to manage the panel so that they are immediately on your side and you have them literally eating out of your hand.

Beware: it is all too common that one of the panel may be up their own arse. Equally, however, I have known panel members to have been more nervous than the candidate and even squabbling amongst themselves in front of the interviewee.

Egos are often at stake on interview panels, so they need to work as hard as you. Often there is a bit of a battle over who can ask the best probing questions to extract information from you, as well as who has the most natural style of interviewing. Like I say, they are often out to impress you, just as you want to impress them, so be conscious that they may try hard to engage with you and be competitive.

Use these five tips if faced with a panel interview and you will be a real winner.

Tip 1: Get the preparation sorted

Prepare exactly as you would if you were attending a series of one-on-one interviews. Be nosey and make sure you find out prior to the interview, if you can, who will be on the panel. Check out their job titles and roles within the organisation. If you have an 'inside' contact, then grill them so that you can find out what the turn ons and offs are for each member of the panel.

Research the company rigorously in the normal manner, and take in everything from its structure and financial position to its main business and product range. If the panel consists of members from different departments, make sure you find out about their respective areas of responsibility. This will help you answer any questions they decide to throw at you. If it is a public sector interview, ensure that you understand the organisation's stance on engaging with the public as they place a lot of emphasis on this as well as equal opportunities. And always prepare yourself mentally. Visualise the flow of the panel interview: see, hear and feel yourself answering the questions with ease, self-confidence and a strong rapport.

Tip 2: Something for everyone

When you research and prepare for the panel interview, you need to be able to have ammunition to turn on all the members. This means you need to have something to offer each of them. Equip yourself with examples that showcase your wide range of capabilities. For example, as someone applying for an HR Manager role you will of course describe what HR strategies you have implemented in your experience, but if the finance director is on the panel you will be well advised to describe their bottom-line effectiveness. Demonstrate your abilities so that all panel members feel part of the conversation. For instance, if the head of IT was on the panel in this example the applicant could show that they understand the application and impact of IT in HR perhaps by talking about manpower information systems.

Tip 3: Chemical connection

Panel interviews are often impersonal because you won't have long to build up a rapport with each person. Therefore your introductions are crucial. As soon as you walk into the room, take a moment to connect with everyone who is on the panel by shaking their hand, greeting them by name and making good eye contact with them. Let the eyes smile, and mentally imagine you are connecting deeply with each panel member. Avoid the embarrassment factor if you find one of them particularly attractive. Save that for a later date!

Tip 4: Engage

Just because there are more of them doesn't mean you can only speak when addressed. Don't feel intimidated by their number. Of course avoid at all costs interrupting or talking over panel members, but don't be afraid to initiate conversation. For instance, you may want to bring in something that you have read.

As the questions start to be asked, answer them in a succinct manner. Be open and honest about your answers and always give examples.

Talk to all the members of the panel and not just the person who asked the question. The answer you give has to be the right one for each panel member. If there is one particular panel member who everyone else seems to agree with, be sure to impress him or her. Do make eye contact with the others as you speak, to involve them in your communication.

If one of the panel members looks a misery, then don't let this faze you. Perhaps they are the kind of person who never gets excited full stop. It may even be a silly tactic they are adopting to see how you cope under pressure. There are still some very strange 'good cop/bad cop' practices out there.

Make sure you massage the ego of all panel members. Give them respect and treat all their questions seriously and with interest and understanding.

Tip 5: Esteem machine

You know you best, and understand what you have to offer and why you should be top of the list at the end of the panel process. You must appreciate yourself and value what you have to offer. Hold your head high and see yourself as a rare item, as opposed to one that is 'mass-market' that tends to be marked down in a sale. Let go of any inferior feelings you have as you look at the range of eyes glaring at you across the table. You are an equal, so get that into your head and hold that head high. Practise the belief techniques from Chapter 6 to help your self-esteem go sky high. Never feel inferior during the interview, and remember the interview panel members are human and fallible just like you. Fear not!

Be sure to think about how you want to be perceived, and imagine you are successful in this. It is also useful to think about all the things that could go wrong, such as one of the miserable sods being difficult or unresponsive. In this case, just imagine being relaxed, composed, getting things back on track naturally and confidently and it will happen.

Character action

Do remember it is OK to show individuality and communicate in a way that shows you have character. Of course you aren't going to connect with all the interview panels you attend, but it is important you remain you. After all, would you really want to work for an organisation where you couldn't express yourself the way you want to? 'I am what I am . . .'

Real Life

Dale

After an initial interview for a job as a regional operations director with a print company, Dale was asked to complete a psychometric test and then be interviewed by the company's board and the person who was retiring from the operations director post.

Dale, who was 39, came to me knowing that he'd face a rigorous process to land the job he'd dreamt of, and he wanted to have an edge over rivals.

He was outwardly confident and smart in his appearance, but his biggest flaw was not listening to other people who were talking to him, including me. It took several sessions for me to convince him that this was a weakness, and that he should listen to others and use their information and input to make his responses and questions sharp.

To get over his flaw, we practised some simple observation and feedback sessions where I asked him to monitor what I was saying and I would ask him questions about it later. After a couple of sessions, Dale had developed his listening skills so he could retain key facts from my interactions with him and come back with answers that showed he was engaged by me and interested.

He went on to get the operations director post, and tells me he's changed his own skills to tune into the needs of his team by listening to them.

Rosa

Rosa was a 26-year-old graduate from Durham University, an intelligent and engaging young woman, whose passion was to join the Diplomatic Service.

On paper Rosa was a perfect candidate who had the language skills and academic credentials that got her to a selection day and initial interview. A friend recommended she see me when it became clear that she was absolutely petrified of being interviewed in a panel situation.

Apparently she'd had a couple of bad experiences during interviews in the past and had tended to fall apart if questions got difficult or people were not friendly. I got down to brass tacks with Rosa by explaining that she really needed to toughen up, especially if she wanted to be a high-flyer in the Diplomatic Service.

I worked with her on bolstering her self-belief, and also introduced her to the techniques that can make a person bubble with confidence: projecting the inner smile, looking people in the eyes and talking clearly using tonality that grabs interest. We finished our sessions with a mock panel interview that really gave Rosa a grilling. She understood that people who interview for roles like the one she wanted don't want to be your friend, but they do want to see what you are made of.

She put all the techniques into practice and is now in the Diplomatic Service. Result!!!

Beverley

Beverley wanted to get a promotion, within a very large furniture group, that would see her lead a team of nearly 50 people. At 28, she'd had the experience of leading and managing smaller teams, but she knew this was a big step up for her and that she'd have to convince a panel interview that she could deliver.

She and I worked out a plan that prepared her to deal with the panel's questions. We rehearsed what they might ask and how she could demonstrate that she could make the jump from managing up to ten people to a department of 50. Part of this was preparing with research into the department she wanted to lead, talking to a first line manager contact who knew the department, and finding out what its strengths and weaknesses were.

The 'insider' knowledge put Bev into a position of strength, and she impressed the interview panel with a strategy to develop and mentor the junior managers she would take charge of. Bev is now a divisional director for the company, with a direct responsibility for the performance and success of hundreds of people.

I've shown you that the panel interview isn't something to be afraid of; in fact it's a challenge to rise to and to savour. The process to be a successful candidate picked from a panel interview may seem challenging, but look at it like other interviews where you get the chance to talk to people and shine. Instead of facing one person, it's your chance to impress several at once, so go on and grab it.

Keep my Top Five Tips in mind and you won't go far wrong in being able to get an interview panel onside and convinced that you are the best person to fulfil the job role.

Job Grabber check list

- See the panel as another opportunity to shine
- Keep eye contact with the person who's talking to you
- Let the real you come out
- Treat it as a chance to impress more than one person at once

Kick-ass-essment centre

22

Things have moved on from when our mum or dad had worked somewhere for life, and after a word with the director or manager they got us an 'interview'. No, my dears, you're competing in a tough old world where young people have A levels and degrees coming out of their backsides and it's difficult to separate the wheat from the chaff.

This is why a lot of organisations now put candidates through the 'ordeal' of going to an assessment centre as opposed to merely conducting the traditional interview. A survey commissioned by the Chartered Institute of Personnel and Development found that 47 per cent of employers had used assessment centres in some way to select applicants.

The very words 'assessment centre' may have you quaking in your boots and bring on visions of *The Krypton Factor* crossed with

Gladiators, but let me reassure you that with some preparation and my help you'll be in great shape to do well and shine.

One of the strengths of assessment centres is that they allow a broader range of selection methods to be used in the recruitment process, and let's face it, that can help many who always let themselves down at the interview stage. My view is that assessment centres are nothing to be scared of and in fact they can offer you the chance to shine outside the narrow format of a traditional 'interview for the job' situation.

What happens?

When you are invited to an assessment centre, you will normally attend with a small group of other candidates. During the day you will be given some individual tests and some group activities, to judge your suitability for the job.

Sometimes assessment centres are organised at the company with its own staff, or independent assessors are brought in, or sometimes the tests and activities are run at specialised, dedicated assessment centres.

On the theory side, you will be given paper/computer-based questionnaires and assessed against a number of key competencies which are usually linked in some way to the job you are going for. You will be given a score against each one, which will help the assessor/s gauge how well you would fit into, and grow with, the post you want.

The company will use an assortment of selection methods that will measure your key skills and abilities, and also find out where you have areas for improvement. We all have those, so don't get hung up on the idea that you've got to be perfect.

On a typical assessment day you can expect to be asked to complete:

- Group tasks
- Psychometric tests (these can ask you some strange questions, but be true to yourself when answering them – see section 6 below)
- A presentation given by you
- A structured interview – panel or one-to-one

Preparing well beforehand is obviously vital, so do your research on the post you're applying for, and if it's a new job with a new company, then for God's sake do some research on the whole organisation.

If the company doesn't send you a programme agenda for the assessment day/s, then it is worth calling them to ask for one. Having the programme will help you to prepare with your research and to get your physical and mental states in order, ready to perform brilliantly.

As well as finding out about the company in as much detail as possible, you are well advised to practise delivering a PowerPoint presentation, take some mock psychometric tests and always make sure that you get a good 8-hour sleep the night before!

How to perform in style at the assessment centre

1 The arrival

You already know that you need to look the bees bollocks, so on the day get up early to make yourself look groomed and professional. Smell fragrant, not OTT. Take time to choose a suit or outfit that sends out the right signal – you're not auditioning for *Britain's Next Top Model* so forget outlandish make-up, hair and clothes that you'd go clubbing in.

Arrive 15 minutes before the day starts and affirm in your own mind that you are calm and confident. Walk tall and smile with your eyes as well as your mouth, but don't overdo it. You don't want to look too cheesy.

Sit with the others and keep your posture straight. If you are invited to have a coffee or tea, then make sure you have one or ask for water. Be polite, and remember that you are a winner: someone who is at ease with themselves and others, and someone who is unique. Finally, never, ever yawn. It may sound obvious, but you would be amazed how often candidates do that, thinking it's showing that they are relaxed. Not only is it rude, but it will most definitely get you off to a bad start.

2 The company presentation

It is quite possible that the assessment centre will start with a presentation about the company and its activities. Make sure you look interested, but again don't go over the top by sitting forward and asking questions every minute. Allow the presenter to talk while you look genuinely interested and send subliminal thoughts. In your mind, as you gain eye contact with him/her, send the thoughts that you both get on; that you like each other and that you know he or she wants to know you more. Let the eyes send those messages – but avoid horny thoughts as it may scare them off!

At the end of the presentation ask a couple of questions if you are certain the answers haven't already been covered. Don't be embarrassed to ask obvious questions, but do make sure the question is relevant.

3 Group activities

The assessment centre normally includes a group task of some description. This may include building a tower with playing cards or Lego pieces, or you may be handed a scenario where you are lost at sea and you have a load of items that have been salvaged from your sinking ship. The idea is for you and others to rank items in order of priority to help you survive. I know your Mac lipstick is important, girls, but get the priorities straight and show that you can lead and work as a team player.

As you carry out the activities, be aware that the assessors aren't necessarily looking out for the one candidate who can talk the most (often pissing other people off), but are looking for the one who offers a constructive contribution, demonstrates they can listen, shows empathy and promotes the ideas of others.

Sometimes each person is asked to play a certain part; sometimes there is a free discussion. If you are asked to take on the role of leader or chairman, be sure you plan and keep control of the discussion. Whatever your role is, you need to be assertive at appropriate times and show that you do listen. Do show empathy, but also use the 'I' statement to underline your convictions and point of view.

4 Delivering a presentation

Sometimes the organisation will ask candidates to prepare a presentation in advance of the assessment centre. However, you may be asked to do so on the day. If you are not given a topic in advance of the assessment centre, I would advise you to prepare something as a practice run, which you could also use in case you are given a free choice on the day.

So follow my framework for preparing a presentation as set out below:

i *Confirm the overall aim of your presentation.* For example, the overall aim may be to 'explain the critical success factors of a sales professional' or to 'explain what makes an inspirational leader' or to 'discuss classroom management in the teaching profession'. Remember, your aim is to be sure of the thread that must run through your presentation. If you run off on tangents, then there's a good chance you will lose your audience and bore them to death.

ii *Design the objectives of the presentation.* Here you list what the audience will have received at the end of the presentation. Always start the objectives with a statement that reads 'At the end of this presentation you will have . . .'. For the first example it could be: 'At the end of this presentation you will have a. knowledge of the critical success factors for sales professionals, b. knowledge of the skills required to achieve the critical success factors, and c. knowledge of the behaviours that will help achieve the critical success factors.' For the next example: 'At the end of this presentation you will have a. understood what makes an inspirational leader, b. appreciated the benefits of inspirational leadership, and c. gained an insight into how inspirational leadership adds value to the bottom line.' Finally, for our third example: 'At the end of this presentation you will a. have an understanding of strategies to manage the classroom, b. have a knowledge of how classroom management strategies are conducive to the learning environment, and c. have an appreciation of the impact classroom management strategies have on exam results.'

iii *Draft a headline for each objective.* Use a slide or two of PowerPoint for each headline. The headline should relate to each objective. For example, if you were preparing the presentation on inspirational leadership, then the headlines for the objectives may be 'What makes an inspirational leader'; 'Benefits of inspirational leadership' and finally 'Inspirational leadership adding value'. In other words, you paraphrase your objectives. Once you have your headlines you can, in bullet point fashion, put down your key points. These key points will act as prompts which save you from making the mistake of reading word for word from a script.

iv *Conclusions and Recommendations.* The final part of your presentation contains your conclusions and, if appropriate, your recommendations. Conclusions are the key summary points from your presentation. It is useful to have three conclusions. If appropriate, end the presentation on providing recommendations to your audience. You should have between three and six recommendation points.

6 Psychometric tests

There are three types of psychometric tests:

i *Ability tests.* These will have correct and incorrect answers, and are designed to test your verbal, logical, numerical and analytical abilities.

ii *Aptitude tests.* These also have correct and incorrect answers, but they will measure how well you are likely to perform in the job. For example, for a management role you may be requested to role play a management scenario.

iii *Personality tests.* These help to draw conclusions about your behavioural characteristics. For example, are you an extrovert or an introvert? Or are you logical or creative? Remember there is no right and wrong answer to these questions, so always be honest. Never fake the personality test as many of them are designed to catch out people who are bullshitters and fakes.

Of course, before your assessment you can practise ability tests, and I would recommend you to get hold of some of them. You can also improve your chances of attaining good results by reading a quality newspaper or some stimulating books. In addition, practise your numeric skills. For information on how to obtain ability tests contact the British Psychological Society – www.bps.org.uk.

I have also recently come across a useful tool called MAP Assessment which has been developed to assess people at management level. It's a mix of personality and ability tests that measure someone's capabilities as a manager against tens of thousands of others who have gone through the assessment process. It's useful as a really accurate benchmarking tool if you are considering moving into a management level job, or you are a manager and want to find out where and how you can improve your competencies, perhaps to win a promotion, or just to impress your boss!

MAP Assessment is good because it is a truly objective method of assessing an individual's management potential and capabilities. It will also go on to point you in the direction of coaching and online resources to enhance your skills. You can find out more at www.map-assessment.co.uk.

Before you sit the assessment centre tests, avoid panicking. If you panic, your intellectual functioning will be seriously inhibited. Before you begin, take some deep breaths and imagine the anxiety drifting out of your fingers and out of your toes. Do this for a few minutes and you will find it helps to clear your mind and develop a calm concentrated focus.

As you sit, keep your cool and follow all of the instructions given on the test paper. Make sure that you read the instructions fully. Take your time as you read, so that no mistakes are made in terms of what you have to do. If you are unsure of anything, don't be afraid of asking the assessor for assistance. Ensure that you distribute your time equally between the questions as you want to ensure you answer them all if possible. If unsure, then leave the question and move on.

You can always come back to it later. If you finish early, go back over your answers, and also have a stab at any you have left not done.

Now you've walked through the assessment centre process with me, I know you will be prepared, focused, confident and ambitious to get selected for the job you want. The assessment centre is there to find out about you as a 'rounded' product, so, if you feel you have weaknesses in some areas, don't think that you'll get them picked out and you won't make the cut. It's often the case that the assessment centre tests will be used to find out the variety of skills that you can contribute, and the assessors will know that most people are better at some things than others.

Job Grabber *check list*

- Accept assessment centres as common practice and as a chance to stand out from the crowd
- Do your job/company research
- Check out the kick-ass-essment centre tips

The job offer – acceptance or two-finger salute?

23

OK, you've beaten the competition and hit the mark, and you are now being offered a job. Your instinct may tell you to snap up the offer straight away, but, before you climax with joy, some careful consideration is needed. In my experience, it's wise to reflect and consider the offer and the pros and cons of taking the job.

The decision may seem easy, but it's not always the case. Weighing it up needs close examination. The worst thing to do is trot into a new job, stay two days, then bugger off because you detest the sight of your boss who keeps looking at your crotch or cleavage, or you justifiably have a distaste for the miserable sods you are working with, and what's more you realise the place is like a morgue and full of sick and sour office politics. However, you should have got inklings of this *before* you accepted the job offer.

If you don't carefully consider the situation, then you could easily be jumping from the frying pan into the fire, so we need to take a look at how you can evaluate if the job really is for you or not. Give this all the time it needs, and don't be scared that you have to decide asap or the job or promotion will go to someone else. That's nonsense as they clearly want *you*.

It's good to know that most organisations will allow you a few days to mull over the offer before you accept, so study my evaluations carefully. Also, don't be pushed or pressured into taking a job because the employer is desperate to have you. They may have a hidden agenda, or skeletons in the cupboard they haven't told you about.

Evaluation 1: The new boss

The new boss has the power to make your time in the new job awesome or totally crap. Once the job offer has been made, if you have any reservations, ask to meet the boss at the office where you will be based to suss him or her out. The last thing you want is to be working for a total pervert who is more interested in your body bits, or someone who is a miserable fucker who fails to smile and replies, when you politely offer a good morning, 'What's so bloody good about it?'

Use your common sense and brain to gauge their character, intelligence and how you think they will operate. You know best the type of people you like to work for and with, so use your noggin and make sure they fit the bill.

If you have any gut feeling that this new boss is going to be a drag to work for, or is up their own arse so much it stinks, then turn it down. The gut feeling is your unconscious mind saying 'Keep away!' Score him or her out of ten. Anything below 8, walk away, my darlings.

Evaluation 2: The new team

When you go and see the boss, it is also a good time to check out the people you will be working with. Are you greeted with a warm smile and offers of tea or coffee, or are you faced with a heap of sad sacks whose main interest is getting though the daily grind with breath still in their bodies? And if there are too many potential team colleagues looking at you as if they were the Gestapo, then run for your life.

Once you have the job offer, if you do have concerns about the team, then call the boss and arrange to go in for a meeting close to lunch time. Explain that you would be keen to have lunch with some of the team whilst you are there. Check out the workplace/office environment and vibe. If it is a case of all heads down until they rise robotically at 1 o'clock for lunch, then I would forget it unless of course you enjoy a prison chain-gang style of working. As you go through the lunch with the team, weigh up your experience. Any score less than 7 out of ten, walk away and think that you've had a lucky escape.

Evaluation 3: Goal alignment

I want you now to have a look into the future, about five or ten years. Does this job really align itself to what you want and what you think you will be doing years from now? Will it help develop your skills, or contribute to a natural career progression to that goal? OK, the new job may not directly relate and that is fine. However, it needs to offer something that will make a contribution to your ambition. For example, if your goal is to move into teaching eventually and you take a new job as a customer service team leader, that will be fine as the new role will offer you the opportunity to develop your leadership qualities and your communication and organisational skills. Work out in your own mind what the new role will provide. If you doubt there is much alignment, then turn it down and put it down to you being a shit hot interviewee.

Weigh up if this job will also give you a chance to experience things you haven't experienced and learn things you don't already know. What are the training opportunities? Oh yes, for those of you who aspire to become a bigwig, does there seem to be a good chance that you'll be moving on up in the organisation over time?

Never accept the job because you think you are supposed to, because your partner, friends or family want you to. You must consider your own needs first, so yes, consult them, but don't let them force you into taking it. It's your life!

Evaluation 4: The business culture

Weigh up what the company or organisation is really like. Do the people work well together, do people get involved, is there a sense of engagement? Being on the outside, this is difficult to judge. That said, you will have picked a few things up from the interview stages. Again, if you have any concerns try to find out by asking around or calling your new boss and discussing it openly.

Think hard about the interview you had and what you know about the potential employer. Does their culture and mission fit with your own character, ambitions and vision?

Go online and read through the literature on the company. Good signs will be if the organisation talks about its people positively and proudly. Does it seem employee focused? If in doubt, here are a few questions to ask of people at the company – if you didn't at the interview stage – before accepting the new job:

- What is the organisation's view on career development?
- Are there opportunities to get involved in company activities?
- What is it like to work here?
- Is it evident that the company cares about, and supports, the people it employs?
- How would you describe the personality of the company?
- How long do people normally stay with the company?

Again, before you sign on the dotted line and accept the job offer, be clear that you want to be a part of that company or organisation and what it does and what it stands for. Any major reservations, then walk on by.

Evaluation 5: The job

Now the interview is over and you have been a Get Off Your Arse role model in grabbing the job, take some time to really think through if the job is going to interest you. Does it match your interests? Is it going to stimulate your brain and stretch you? Will it make good use of your skills? If in doubt, and you score the job low on these points, then forget it and move on to your next application. If your brain and gut say that it ticks the boxes you think are important, then accept it.

As well as checking that the job's responsibilities and skills fit with *you*, you must also be up for the hours *it* will demand. If you want a regular 37.5 hours a week Monday to Friday, then be sure that that is what the job offers. Many jobs these days require a degree of flexibility, including working on a Saturday and also Sundays, so that deadlines and business goals can be met. Be sure to consider the effect the work will have on your personal life.

Evaluation 6: Salary checker

When the organisation makes the offer, this will usually include salary details. Remember, if you are not happy with what is offered, there is normally room for negotiation. However, you need to be aware of what you are worth. Be realistic, but don't undervalue yourself. Good research will help determine if the offer is fair: websites to aid that research include www.totaljobs.com, www.monster.co.uk and www. reed.co.uk

In conjunction with the salary checkers, you need to consider your experience and qualifications. If, for example you have ten years' job-related experience and are professionally qualified, these variables will give you power in the negotiation if the salary is below the national average. If, on the other hand, you have a couple of years' experience and do not possess the appropriate professional qualifications, then don't be greedy. Also, consider supply and demand. If vacancies are plentiful for your specific chosen vocation, with few candidates to fill them, your power is greater. Above all, remember it is about proving your worth.

Finally, check out when salary reviews take place. Most employers will evaluate your performance annually. Don't be afraid to ask if there is an opportunity for a salary review sooner, say after the first six months, if you feel strongly about it. Only accept when you are happy with the package. If you take a job and start feeling you are being undervalued and underpaid, you will be de-motivated from the word go and will probably come off worst.

Real Life

Charlotte

Charlotte was 43 and desperate to move jobs. She was employed as a business management lecturer in a local further education college, but she was unhappy with the culture of the employer, describing the organisation as hierarchical and hampered by a blame culture.

Charlotte applied for similar posts with other colleges in the region, and was offered a new position as senior lecturer in the business studies department of a large sixth form college.

She wanted to be confident that she was making the right decision, so before accepting the job she decided to have a meeting with the person who would be her manager. She also asked to spend a day of her own time meeting other members of the academic team. The time she spent reassured her that she wasn't doing the frying pan into the fire shuffle, and she felt comfortable that the culture and team were positive.

One thing she was not happy with, however, was the salary offered, so she negotiated a further increment on the pay scale by explaining she had 15 years' experience and an MBA.

Charlotte took a full week before deciding to accept the senior lecturer post, and now loves the job and the people she's working with and for.

Keith

Keith was 32 and employed as a distribution manager. He was very happy with his employer, having worked there for four years, but he wanted to move on to experience a new sector and develop new skills.

After some searching around, applications and interviews, he was offered a group distribution manager's job with an online retailer.

The offer included an £8,000 pay rise and very nice company car, but something didn't fit right and Keith's gut instinct was that something was missing.

He decided to ask to meet with the Operations Director of the business, who he found to be arrogant, chauvinistic and clearly suffering from small-dick syndrome.

The other members of the team he met were fine, but he felt a sense of fear and unease in the department. When he came away from the meeting, he knew that his gut feeling would win the day and he decided he could not work for someone who conducted themselves like an arrogant arsehole.

He decided to decline the offer of the job, but the company then increased the salary offer. Again, he declined. Keith was confident that he had made the right decision. He would move on and apply for another role, but would continue to take his time and not jump at the first 'fantastic' offer that was made.

I trust that you'll understand from reading the advice and the real life example of Keith that what seems like a 'golden ticket' may turn out to be a poisoned chalice that will make your life miserable.

Steve Miller

Taking a new job is a major life-changing decision, so you simply must get it right. I don't want you to ignore this advice and become the pogo-stick job candidate who's got a CV full of shit excuses and poor decisions. Be tough, and just say No if that's what you think is right.

Job Grabber *check list*

- Weigh the offer up carefully
- Evaluate the job offer
- Remember the job isn't for life, but it's not just for a couple of months either
- Grab the golden ticket if it's real gold

Fitting in – the first few days and weeks

So you have the job offer and you've made your acceptance; it's now time to prepare for the first day and beyond. As the new girl/guy on the block you are the one who is the unknown, the one who has to find out where the loos and the coffee-making facilities are.

The first day and first few weeks are critical as you need to get used to the new environment and mark your territory – not like a cat or dog; I mean that you need to understand where you fit in. So what can be done to make sure that your face does fit, that you develop sound relationships and become part of the territory?

We'll take a look at the practical steps that can be taken to make your transition smooth.

Step 1: The week before

Try and take some time off between leaving your current job and starting the next, ideally a week. This will help with mentally separating the old and the new, and will declutter your mind. It will also give you a chance to recharge your batteries, although I don't want you going into your new job like the Duracell Bunny and annoying the crap out of everyone.

Leaving behind old colleagues can prove stressful, and you may feel bereaved for a time, so it is really important to make that mental transition and break from your previous employer. Let's face it, you spend a high proportion of your life at work, and, even if the previous work relationships weren't great, you need time out before starting the new job because you have got so used to them.

Use this time well. Do some research on the organisation you will be joining. Perhaps check out if anyone knows your future colleagues, and if they do then why not get them to introduce you. Then at least on day one you will see a familiar friendly face.

Plan your impact for day one. What will you wear? Be sure to get your image spot-on for the first day because, as you know, I believe that the first impressions you create will be the ones that stick. It is so difficult to turnaround a poor first impression, so plan it thoroughly, making sure the clothes you choose look immaculate and professional. Plan your travel to work: check out the best routes to take, and how long it will take to get there. There's no way you want to start your first day late, as this will make a terrible impression.

Preparation is crucial. You will be glad you have done all this, because you will start your first day relaxed and confident.

Step 2: The first few days

Set the alarm the night before the first day to wake up at least ninety minutes before you leave home. Put on the outfit we've discussed, the one that makes you shine, the one that makes you feel like a star, and instantly makes you feel confident and self-assured.

Make sure you have breakfast before you leave as we don't want your tummy rumbling in an early meeting. Oh, and please clean your teeth well, and if you suffer from bad breath then take a mouthwash or some breath freshener capsules. The last thing you want is the whisper that you are the newby who stinks. On the way to work be cautious, as you never know who you will spot when driving. Can you imagine picking your nose in the car and being spotted by a driver on the dual carriageway only to meet them as a new colleague when you arrive at work – or getting involved in road rage, and shouting to the other driver to fuck off, and then finding them next to you at your first meeting. Good rapport? Erm, perhaps not.

As you draw up to your new place of work, take a deep breath and walk in the door with a warm smile on your face. Yes, smile please! We want you looking as if you are delighted to be there. As you meet the person who greets you, make sure you have good eye contact and tell them you are pleased to meet them. If you've already met them, perhaps through a first interview, try and remember something personal about them to show that you listened to what they said and that you're interested in them.

As you are introduced to people, be polite and friendly, no matter who they are or who you think they are. If you are taking on a senior role, remember you don't want to be known as the one who is up their own arse and thinks they are 'above everyone else'. You want the co-operation and commitment of your new team, so forget any aloofness.

When you meet the people you are going to be working with, feel free to ask any questions. This will show you are genuinely interested in them, and people quite enjoy helping others. It is also good to let your new colleagues know that you will catch up with them later if you don't have the time immediately, so say it. And forget sounding and looking as though you know everything; know-alls fail pretty quickly, so please don't project yourself like that.

Do your best to recall people's names from day one. If you find yourself in a situation where you have forgotten someone's name, then the best solution is to admit it, apologise, and ask their name again.

Not everyone is blessed with a photographic memory, so consider taking notes. This will certainly help you to remember policies, systems and the names of key personnel.

Step 3: The first few weeks and months

It's great to take with you the experiences gained from your previous job and to use that knowledge appropriately, but do remember that each organisation will have its own way of doing things. The first few weeks is not the time to storm in and change the way things are done. You will just piss people off. If there is something you feel needs changing for the better, then suggest it and discuss it with colleagues at the appropriate time and place such as a management planning meeting or at a one-to-one with your boss. Don't steam ahead and do it regardless.

Another thing, avoid at all costs saying the words 'We didn't do it like that in my old company.' People will react negatively and probably think 'Well, fuck off back there then.'

In the first few weeks you may fit in really well and adjust to your new environment quickly, but for some it takes a little longer. Continue to ask relevant questions, so that you are seen as someone who checks things out and you do things right first time, being sure of what you are doing.

Ensure that you maintain a friendly persona, and if you manage people be consistent and demonstrate a firm but fair approach with *all* the people who report to you. Don't storm into the first meeting you chair, making changes too quickly. Consult first and then act on your decision, communicating the reasons for it.

Get to know your colleagues well and listen more than you talk. Show people you are genuinely interested in them, rather than shouting about yourself. Don't be afraid to ask a colleague to join you for lunch, but make sure you don't express the request as though it is a come on!

As the weeks pass, pay attention to the grapevine but never contribute to it. Forget joining in with gossip, otherwise you will be labelled as someone who cannot be trusted. Equally important is stopping any notion about complaining about your new boss, even if they are an arse, and never slag off the organisation. The same goes for talking about your old company as word will spread that you are a serial whinger. Put effort into good time-keeping and punctuality, and be sure to volunteer for the occasional project: showing you have a positive attitude will go down well.

I would suggest that you seek feedback from your new boss after a few weeks in the job. Ask for specifics, and check out what is going well and where improvements can be made. If you are managing people, then have a sit-down breakfast meeting after the first month and share with the team your findings and any changes you propose to make. At the same time, involve the team by asking for their comments and listen to them. Explain that some of your decisions may not be the most popular; however, you are acting in the interests of them and the business for the future. The secret here is to stay firm but remain warm.

As the weeks turn into months, it is also useful to have identified and engaged with a mentor. If you are a fresh-faced graduate, this is particularly crucial for your development. Perhaps a member of the senior management team outside your department would be a good choice. Don't be afraid to ask senior staff to help to mentor you, as this shows that you've got initiative. Mentoring has many benefits: it is a great sounding board and offers guidance for your personal and professional development.

As the months go by, make sure that you stay organised and focused, and set your goals. This is usually in consultation with your line manager, but you may have personal goals such as improving your image or assertive communication skills. When you write down your personal goals, post them everywhere at home so that you see them daily.

As a proactive job-grabber, I would hope that you will have been networking with key people in the organisation. Take advantage of every opportunity to do this, so you become well known. Attend training courses, outside seminars, breakfast meetings, the list is endless. Get your face associated with being a go-getter and with being with the right people. Be sure to grow your network, as these people will both support and promote your career.

Real Life

Katherine

Katherine was a 38-year-old newly appointed senior Finance Manager.

Following redundancy from her City job, she decided to move from professional practice into a public sector organisation. She planned to have two weeks off before joining the local authority where she'd got the new job, so that she could fully prepare herself.

She did further research on the organisation and ensured she became familiar with its financial systems and budgets. The finances didn't look particularly healthy, and Katherine was determined to make a difference and turn things around.

On joining the organisation, she met each member of her team one by one, ensuring that she listened well and took her time assessing each person's performance. She made sure she came across as a leader who was fair, and demonstrated a genuine interest in all of the team.

Personally, she felt the department was in a shambles, but didn't act in haste and start shouting that things had to change. In her first month, she made sure that she continued to ask questions to get feedback from all her colleagues before reaching any conclusions.

In her second month, Katherine did a business presentation to the team about her observations, and proposed recommendations to improve systems and processes. She consulted with the team members, and then, after another month, implemented her plans.

To this day Katherine says that if she had barged in all guns blazing she would have lost co-operation from her team, and implementing decisions would have been much more difficult. I have to agree. You need the people you work with to be on your side, especially if you have to lead changes that impact on the way that they work.

Isobelle

At 32, nurse Isobelle was moving home with her family and going to work at a completely different hospital. She had her own plan in mind to fit in with her new colleagues: before she moved she made contact with a friend who knew a nurse at the new hospital where she would be based.

Isobelle was introduced to this new colleague, and asked if she could meet her for coffee at the hospital. This helped her to go into the new role with confidence on day one, as she already had a friendly face to meet who could help show her the ropes.

On the first day, Isobelle made sure that she was warm and friendly to everyone and listened more than she talked. She also asked a different colleague each day of the first week if she could join them for lunch, and the professional relationships and contacts blossomed quickly.

Talking to quite a few people in this first week, Isobelle found out that there was a lot of politics on her ward, but she made the conscious decision not to get involved. She also felt that there were some bad practices on the ward, but said nothing. She decided to wait for a few months, then she would gradually highlight some of the issues that she felt needed sorting out.

Jay

A 22-year-old business studies graduate, Jay was joining a construction company as part of the business development team. He had no practical experience and was very aware that graduates were often treated with more than a little suspicion.

To make the right impact, Jay carefully planned what he would wear: a well-cut suit, tie and well-polished shoes. On his first day, he met each new colleague with a warm introduction, and made sure that he asked them questions, rather than suggesting he was the new know-all 'intelligent' kid on the block and acting like a walking text book.

He asked if he could sit with a number of team members, so that he could learn from them. This was very well received. By the end of the first week, Jay was already a member of the family, so to speak. On the Friday he asked if anyone wanted to go for a drink after work, and was pleased when four of his new colleagues agreed to go with him.

Jay continued to grow in confidence as the weeks passed. He ensured he remained punctual, and when he felt under the weather he was determined he would not take the day off.

He also continued to develop relationships, and realised that it was the little things that mattered, for example making coffee and tea for his colleagues, as well as asking if he could help to support certain team members.

Two months into the new job, Jay was very popular. His personality was infectious and he was a great guy to have on board. His boss organised for one of the directors to become his mentor, and a personal development plan was designed to ensure he continued to grow with the business.

Jay is still with the company, was recently promoted to team leader, and is now a role model who works closely with new graduates who join the company.

Job Grabber _check list_

- Go through the practical steps
- Plan your impact and gradually make your presence felt
- Make the right connections as you progress
- Fit into the team or structure

Six weeks
to turn the
'dream' into
'reality'

Going through the book you will have picked up that I like people to make decisions and not to dilly dally all day long about what colour socks they are going to wear or will they look better with highlights or lowlights. However, you also know that I want you to take your time before grabbing that job, to carefully weigh up what's in it for you (will it feed your pocket *and* your soul?), to decide what you want from life and what's going to work for you before you jump in and go for it.

You have decided to take responsibility and forget lame excuses and procrastination. You've been with me in this book so that you can sort out one of the most important areas of your life: your job, your career, your vocation, call it what you will. I know it will have stirred up your emotions; perhaps it has made you take stock of a shitty situation that you are in and that you can now change for the better, or it has simply given you a boot in the pants to grab hold of your ambition and get exactly what you want from your job.

I want you to know that I am really proud of you because you are obviously a doer: you want to make it happen – and that is what successful people do. They don't sit around 'waiting for things to happen', they do it for themselves and they do it now. Like you, they go out of their way to create chances and opportunities, to be in the right place at the right time rather than hoping things will simply fall into place for them.

I too had to make this particular success journey, and I had to realise it was time to get off my arse and make it happen. It might be a bit of a cliché, but one day, about five years ago, I woke up and said to myself 'Miller, it's time you stopped dreaming about being an entrepreneur' – and, boy, did I have one of my Just Fucking Do It (JFDI) episodes. My business interests have grown and I have earned a national reputation as the Life Bitch, 'The Gordon Ramsay of Life Style Gurus', 'Britain's Toughest Life Coach' etc etc. And do you know what? – it feels bloody marvellous.

My secret isn't really a secret because you have done it too; you have decided that you want to change your life by grabbing hold of the job that you really want to do. Like me, you have decided to get off your arse and learn to take control by building your self-belief and using common sense. People might think: If it's just common sense, why do I need to read about it? Well, the truth is that most of us have lost touch with what common sense is. That's why I may sound a little 'bitchy', but it's for your own good that I remind you of what's going to take you forward and turn dreams into action and reality.

You've got this far, you know that I don't tolerate waffle, and you can see that I haven't given you any – just straight-talking advice. The reason, I hear you ask? We both want a result, not tomorrow but today. Setting out to get your dream job means first that you make it your job to find a new job.

I want you to plan the next six weeks immediately. Schedule carefully what you will do day-by-day, week-by-week to make your 'dream job' into a 'reality job'. The actions have to be carried out on a daily basis to grab that dream job in six weeks flat.

In this final chapter I will share with you a real-life six-week strategy to nail that new job. This particular strategy was designed by Danielle, a regular client of mine, who was very hungry to move on to a new job. She bought herself a notebook which she grandly called her 'Life Bitch New Job Journal', and then sat down and planned a day-by-day weekly strategy to make sure she achieved what she wanted.

Grab that dream job!
Danielle's Plan – a real-life strategy

Week 1

- Day 1: Complete the skills audit and identify all the transferable skills I have to offer a new employer.
- Day 2: Consider my next move carefully. Do I want to move to a big fish or a little fish? Complete a pros and cons assessment for each.
- Day 3: What job do I really, really want? Follow what the Life Bitch tells me to consider, otherwise I may jump from the frying pan into the fire and get my ass burnt.
- Day 4: Think through the best way to make my escape. I want to leave on good terms with my current employer as

I will need a good reference and one day may want to return.

- Select what belief systems I will use to increase my confidence and start practising it this week.

Week 2

- Dust off my old CV and review it. Redesign it following the Get Off Your Arse guidelines.
- Once I have done this, find someone who can check over the CV for me. It will be good to seek out a few professional opinions.
- Draft a punchy and impactful covering letter to accompany my CV.
- Email Steve to see what he thinks of my CV.
- Once my CV is selling me well, send it to selected employment agencies and head hunters as well as any other job opportunities I spot that align themselves closely to my needs.

Week 3

- Think through and write down the questions a recruitment agency or prospective new employers will ask me. These questions need to be about me as a person but also questions designed to check out my technical suitability to perform the job.
- Once I have written down the questions, write down some answers that I will be comfortable saying to the interviewer. I must remember it is important to offer examples to justify my answers.

- Think what I will wear to impress the interviewer/s. Go shopping for a new suit as the ones I have are not the most fashionable. It would also be good to buy a new fragrance. [If you are a man, buy a new tie to help dress up the new suit.]
- Contact a good hair stylist as image is going to be so important and at the moment my hair is a bit bland. I will budget £50 for a stylist.
- It has been years since I had an interview, so I will need to practise rapport building with a friend.

Week 4

- Practise selling myself using good posture, voice and eye contact. I will do this in front of the mirror in the bedroom and then in front of my partner as I know they will offer me honest feedback.
- I need to get a second opinion so I will ask a friend to observe me selling myself. I will value their opinion.
- Continue to do the belief system exercises so that I feel really confident. I will do these in the evening before I go to bed. I want my belief to be rock solid and these techniques will make that happen.
- Write down the three questions that I will ask the interviewer, so that I get them into my mind. I need to remember them.
- Read the chapter on assessment centres, as I think there is a chance I will be required to attend one.

Steve Miller

Week 5

- Practise the design and delivery of a presentation as I do believe I will be asked to do one at the second interview. I will ask my partner and a friend to watch me. And ask them for constructive feedback. I'm determined to do well at this.
- Contact the British Psychological Society and request samples of psychometric tests, so that I can get in some practice.
- Assess how many invites for interviews I am receiving. If necessary, redouble my efforts to identify potential employers that I can send my CV to.
- The date for interviews will be getting close at this stage, so I will continue to do my belief system exercises as I need to be mega confident. I will also visualise being interviewed by more than one interviewer as it is distinctly possible it will be an interview panel.
- Get my partner to ask me the questions I think I will be asked at forthcoming interviews. I will practise some model answers. It is important I practise, so that I feel much more confident.

Week 6

- Have a dress rehearsal for my interviews and practise the interview in as much detail as possible with my partner or friends.
- Get in some early nights. I want to make sure mind and body are fresh. I will also stay off the drink and make sure I am eating healthily.
- Check the routes to interviews, and check out how long it will take me to get there as I don't want to be late.

- Continue to affirm positive belief in myself as I am a winner and *will* be successful.
- Make sure that I recap on my research for the interviews. It's important that I am aware of the organisation's products, services and any recent developments.

You are now in great shape to grab your dream job and I want you to keep your sights on getting where you want to be: on the next step up, doing something more fulfilling, or getting right to the top. I hope you will have in mind what your next move is, whether it's a complete life turnaround to do something exciting and fresh, or a steely determination to take the promotion you deserve. Within six short weeks, or sooner, you could be receiving the job offer that previously was just a pipe dream. If you go through my advice and only get offered a job or promotion that you don't really want, it's simple: don't take it, and then again review what you need to do to get exactly what you want. Don't take second best any more, not for anyone and most of all not yourself. Put on your best smile, tell yourself that your time will come soon, and keep on doing the techniques and processes that will grab onto the dream.

When you get where you want to be when it comes to the dream job or career, be very proud of yourself and hold your head up high because you can tell everyone that you are a winner. You can join the growing army of people who realise that sitting on their rump and expecting great things to happen is no way to get anywhere in life. To get what you want, join my army and spread the word that getting off your arse is the start to many successes in life, and grabbing that dream job is the first one for you.

Get the champagne chilling! It's time that you and yours had a toast to you 'starting that dream job'. Keep on going with your new attitude, because you now know that anything is possible, and when you believe that anything is possible then it can really happen for you.

Job Grabber *check list*

- Make a six-week plan to grab that dream job
- Read Danielle's plan as an example
- Don't take the first job that comes along if it doesn't suit you
- Be proud that you are turning your dream into reality

Appendix:
Where to
find the jobs

Online
There are plenty of national and regional online job search engines that can be tailored to the kind of job, salary and location that you want. Here are a few to start you off:

www.monster.co.uk

www.totaljobs.com

www.redgoldfish.co.uk

www.agencycentral.co.uk (good for recruitment agencies and sector-specific job websites)

www.easyjobs.com

www.jobs.guardian.co.uk

www.jobs.ac.uk (academic, research and scientific)

www.jobseekersuk.net

www.jobrapido.co.uk

www.jobsearch.co.uk

www.clickajob.co.uk

www.thebigchoice.com (student/graduate opportunities and advice)

www.manchester.gumtree.com/jobs

National, regional and local printed media
There are too many papers to list them specifically here, so have a look through different ones to find what's good for your sector: e.g. the *Sunday Times* – great for business appointments, especially if you have several years middle/senior level experience; the *Guardian* on Monday is good for media roles; also check the London *Evening Standard* and the *Scotsman.*

Career advice/job progression
www.jobseekersadvice.com
www.learndirect-advice.co.uk/
www.jobsword.co.uk
www.cvtips.com
www.mapassessment.co.uk

Further reading
A–Z of Careers and Jobs, Susan Hodgson (Kogan Page, 2008)
Career Anchors: Self Assessment, Edgar H. Schein (Jossey Bass, 2006)
Dress to Impress: How a Navy Blazer Changed My Life!, Joyce Nelson Shellhart and Lana Beck (Book Peddlers, 2005)
Great Answers to Tough Interview Questions, Martin John Yate (Kogan Page, 2008)
Practice Psychometric Tests: How to Familiarise Yourself with Genuine Recruitment Tests and Get the Job you Want, Andrea Shavick (How To Books Ltd, 2005)
Ready Made CVs: Winning CVs for Every Type of Job, Lynn Williams (Kogan Page, 2008)
The Guardian Careers Guide, David Williams (Guardian Newspapers Ltd, 2008)